The Citrus Industry

The Citrus Industry

A DOMESTIC AND INTERNATIONAL ECONOMIC PERSPECTIVE

Ronald W. Ward
and
Richard L. Kilmer

 Iowa State University Press / Ames

Ronald W. Ward is a professor in the Food and Resource Economics Department at the University of Florida.

Richard L. Kilmer is an associate professor in the Food and Resource Economics Department at the University of Florida.

© 1989 Iowa State University Press, Ames, Iowa 50010
All rights reserved

Manufactured in the United States of America

First edition, 1989

Library of Congress Cataloging-in-Publication Data

Ward, Ronald W.
    The citrus industry : a domestic and international economic perspective / Ronald W. Ward and Richard L. Kilmer. — 1st ed.
        p. cm.
    Bibliography: p.
    Includes index.
    ISBN 0-8138-0052-8
    1. Citrus fruit industry. I. Kilmer, Richard L., 1943–   . II. Title.
HD9259.C52W37   1989
338.1'74306—dc19   89–11195
                                                                                    CIP

Contents

Acknowledgments

The authors acknowledge the financial support from Mr. Elliott Seabrook of Juice Farms Incorporated. His continuing support to the University of Florida and the Institute of Food and Agricultural Sciences is greatly appreciated. Appreciation is extended to the Economic Research Department of the Florida Department of Citrus and to the Food and Resource Economics Department for making their data files available upon request. The authors commend Ms. Debbie Barstis for her assistance with data collection and tabulation. Any omissions are the responsibility of the authors.

Introduction

A long history of citrus production activities can be found within both the developed and developing parts of the world. One can find citrus products being harvested primarily for local consumption with little to no organized market structure. Production technology is crude and product standards are minimal. In contrast, one can turn to those countries where citrus production is a major agricultural endeavor. Product standards are well defined, complex market structures are in place, and marketing efforts are advanced. It is these latter markets on which this book is focused.

The studies of citrus economics as set forth in this book have two primary goals. First, we have attempted to provide insight into the infrastructure of the citrus industry. The text includes detailed statistics on production, pricing, and related data necessary to understanding how the industry performs. Most of the text focuses on U.S. citrus because of its importance as a world supplier and because of the highly developed nature of the industry. Second, the book provides an excellent case study illustrating the complexities typical of many agricultural markets.

The utilization of citrus has evolved from localized fresh use to highly processed forms with juices entering the world's markets. The supporting institutional structures range from little to no regulation to direct governmental involvement in trade. Consumers generally view the citrus products as having several positive characteristics including health attributes. These characteristics and range of product forms have facilitated considerable efforts to achieve product differentiation as reflected through brand identification. Yet the products reaching the final consumer are similar enough in taste, flavor, color, and overall characteristics that one can develop advertising programs designed to enhance the total demand without regard to brands.

While the text will deal with each phase of the industry, we will in this introduction give a brief overview of the complexities of this industry. The text concentrates almost exclusively on the economics beyond the farm gate and does not deal with production problems. This is not to imply that the production economics problems are of less importance but is intended to provide a framework for dealing more with the overall marketing issues.

Production and Marketing Phases

Citrus production has its start with nursery stocks with seedlings that must be replanted. It generally requires from three to five years before any significant yields can be expected. Yields are measured according to the number of boxes per tree and the juice content that can be extracted from a box of fruit. Yields clearly differ depending on variety, production practices, weather, and production regions. Once harvested, the fruit either enters the fresh marketing channels through the typical packinghouse operations or is diverted to processing. It is the processing phase that offers considerable structural complexity.

Processed fruit initially takes one of two forms. Fresh fruit may be directly processed and packaged into ready-to-serve fruit juices or stored and/or packaged in concentrate form, most often referred to as frozen concentrated orange juice. The form of these processed juices is measured in terms of its "brix" content. "Brix" is simply measuring the sugar and orange solids found in a gallon of juice. For example, a ready-to-serve orange juice in the United States generally has 11.8 degrees brixs. Frozen concentrated orange juice shelved in the retail supermarkets is usually 42 degrees brixs and must be diluted with water to get it to the ready-to-serve level. Juices with higher levels of brixs are referred to as bulk concentrate with the industry standards generally ranging from 58 to 65 degrees brixs. Concentrate may be in retail-size packaging that can be reconstituted by the consumer or it may be in bulk form that requires major reconstitution and repackaging facilities to transform the product to consumable juices.

The development of citrus concentrate in the late forties was the single most important technological change impacting the world's citrus economy. More recently, advancements in the production of bulk concentrate have transformed the total citrus economy by extending the storage life and shipping capabilities. What was once an industry with localized markets has now evolved into a complex structure where citrus juices can be stored, moved, and transformed at points far removed from the initial points of production. Wide-scale importing and exporting are now a real part of the world's trade flows for citrus. Citrus juices can be shipped worldwide and reprocessed at points nearer consumer centers. Also, the potential for achieving specific quality standards is more readily attained through blending practices using different juice sources.

The product flow moves through the vertical market system drawing on a variety of exchange mechanisms. One can find highly organized cooperative structures, oligopolistic behavior among processors, and attempts to impose self-regulations as well as government imposed standards. Cooperatives, joint ventures, market orders, centralized selling, futures markets, and oligopolistic firms all play a role in transforming and distributing the product. Strict quality controls are often self-imposed as well as imposed by government standards. The industry, primarily in the United States, is heavily involved in influencing federal policies that are directly related to the citrus economy. Similar activities can be found among other producing countries.

International trade in processed citrus has produced significant economic changes, especially in the last decade. Florida and Brazil produce most of the bulk concentrate and the United States is a major consuming market. Brazil exports most of its citrus, almost exclusively in bulk concentrate form. In recent seasons, Brazil's exports of concentrate to the United States have accounted for nearly 50 percent of the U.S. supplies of processed orange juice. An increasing volume of these imports enter ports near the major consuming centers where the bulk juice is reconstituted into the ready-to-serve products. Imports and reconstitution of juices outside of Florida have led to major structural changes within the U.S. citrus industry.

Much of the distinction between world suppliers of citrus depends on the utilization patterns. Most of the European Economic Community (EEC), African, and Middle East production is sold in fresh form, whereas Brazil and the United States account for the dominant share of the processing capacity and, hence, the world supply of concentrate. Production seasonality for fresh citrus can clearly change the relative competitive positions during the year. For example, South Africa will have a seasonal advantage during part of the year relative to, say, Spain by the very nature of their different harvest seasons. In contrast, seasonality for processed juices, while important, may be lessened with the continued capability for longer term storage and distribution. The opportunity to offset seasonal production patterns and to meet seasonal demands is greatly enhanced through storage.

An Industry in Transition

Like so much of agriculture in the last decade, the world's citrus economy is in a state of transition. One cannot deal with the resulting economic issues without recognition of those driving forces causing most of the changes. Change is reflected through both product sources, the distribution system, and the consumer's search for product quality and convenience. Six primary contributing factors can be identified as the most important conditions leading to the dynamics of the citrus economy:

- Changes in processing technology leading to increased storability and distribution of commercial grade juices (bulk concentrate)
- Growth of the Brazil citrus industry as a major factor in the world markets for citrus juices
- Impact of significant weather patterns that can in a period of less than 24 hours substantially reduce the expected production and thus transform the total citrus economy for several seasons
- Increasing consumer demand for convenience goods as reflected by the growth of the ready-to-serve orange juice markets
- Endeavor to achieve product differentiation through brand advertising while simultaneously supporting various forms of cooperative promotional efforts, all leading to improved quality
- Shifts in market shares and decision-making authority along with increased government involvement in several citrus producing countries (i.e., U.S. tariff policies, Brazil export pricing policies)

As the reader works through the text, it is useful to recognize the interdependence among these factors, for truly, they are not independent economic forces.

Overview of the Book

In this book our intent is to provide statistics and insight into the economics of this industry. Citrus is of interest in and of itself. However, many of the structural changes noted in the text have broader applications for illustrating the dynamics and complexities of an agricultural industry as it moves into the international marketplace. The citrus industry provides an excellent case study where most forms of structural arrangements can be found.

The book is divided into four major sections. Section 1 deals with the production and utilization of oranges predominantly for the U.S. market. Section 2 addresses demand and price issues while Section 3 deals with market development and overall industry values. Dimensions of international citrus trade are considered in Section 4.

While the book attempts to discuss international market issues relating to citrus, it does have more of a U.S. domestic orientation and draws heavily on Florida statistics. This must be the case since the United States is the most significant consuming market for processed citrus and has such an important role in determining the economic direction of the industry worldwide. As the reader deals with the data, he or she should always keep in mind the changes evolving with the growth of Brazil as a major supplier of orange juice. Economic issues, structural changes, pricing policies, and government policies all center around this evolving role for Brazil.

No book can deal completely with all of the topics and related issues. There are several areas that are only cursorily discussed and in some cases updated data are simply not available. Likewise, important literature concerning many of the foreign markets has likely been omitted. Any omissions are obviously the responsibility of the authors.

Production
and
Distribution

1

Production, Geographical Distribution, and Product Forms

National Citrus Production Trends

The industry analysis and description presented in this chapter are limited to oranges and grapefruit, which account for approximately 90 percent of all U.S. citrus production. Principal commodities excluded are lemons, limes, and minor specialty fruits. The excluded commodities can be readily omitted from the analysis since many of them are marketed within the existing market structure for oranges and grapefruit.

As of 1984–85 the U.S. citrus industry supplied 19.6 percent of the world supply of oranges and 60.8 percent of the grapefruit. This contrasts with the middle fifties, when the United States provided nearly 43.1 percent of the world's oranges and 88.5 percent of the world's grapefruit (Table 1.1). Even though the U.S. share of citrus production has declined, the number of cartons produced in the United States has grown approximately 50 percent since the middle to late fifties. The U.S. share of both products declined somewhat in the early 1980s. These shifting shares are primarily a result of rapid growth in Brazil's citrus production and of severe crop losses from freezes in Florida.

Total U.S. orange acreage increased very little from 1957–58 to 1985–86, with the most pronounced growth occurring in the mid-1960s. Total bearing acreage reached a peak in 1970–71 and has been trending downward since (Table 1.2). Changing acreage and fluctuating yields per acre have resulted in annual supply variations. The average yield trended upward from 1970–71 through 1979–80 and has trended downward since, except for a significant increase in 1985–86.

Total production has followed the same trends. This can be attributed to the freezes in Florida and Texas during the early 1980s. Unlike
oranges, U.S. grapefruit bearing acreage reached its peak in 1979–80
with total production peaking in 1976–77. Bearing acreage has trended
downward since 1979–80 but production has trended downward during
the 1980s as a result of freezing weather in Florida and Texas (Table 1.3).
Only in the last two years has the trend shown signs of an upward
movement.

Table 1.1. World and United States citrus production, 1956-57 through 1984-85.

Crop year[a]	ORANGES[b]			GRAPEFRUIT			TOTAL		
	World	U.S.	U.S.% of world	World	U.S.	U.S.% of world	World	U.S.	U.S.% of world
	Million cartons[c]			Million cartons[c]			Million cartons[c]		
1956-57	635.4	273.8	43.1	101.3	89.6	88.5	736.7	363.4	49.3
1957-58	643.7	222.8	34.6	93.2	79.6	85.4	736.9	302.4	41.0
1958-59	729.8	267.8	36.7	101.5	87.6	86.3	831.3	355.4	42.8
1959-60	749.3	259.7	34.7	99.2	83.2	83.9	848.5	342.9	40.4
1960-61	713.4	243.5	34.1	102.3	86.8	84.8	815.7	330.3	40.5
1961-62	791.3	285.8	36.1	103.2	85.8	36.1	894.8	371.6	41.5
1962-63	748.4	215.3	28.8	89.1	69.5	78.0	837.5	284.8	34.0
1963-64	788.5	194.5	24.7	91.6	68.4	74.7	880.1	262.9	29.9
1964-65	864.4	250.1	28.9	105.5	82.1	77.8	969.9	332.2	34.3
1965-66	934.5	291.9	31.2	121.1	93.4	77.1	1,055.6	385.3	36.5
1966-67	1,148.2	393.6	34.3	143.6	111.8	77.9	1,291.8	505.4	39.1
1967-68	1,018.1	268.6	26.4	120.3	88.1	73.2	1,138.4	356.7	31.3
1968-69	1,190.5	388.8	32.7	144.7	108.3	74.8	1,335.2	497.1	37.2
1969-70	1,269.5	394.7	31.1	150.5	107.8	71.6	1,420.0	502.5	35.2
1970-71	1,399.4	406.9	29.1	176.8	121.1	68.5	1,576.2	527.2	33.4
1971-72	1,454.6	414.0	28.5	184.5	128.3	69.5	1,639.1	542.3	33.1
1972-73	1,648.5	477.8	29.0	192.9	131.3	68.1	1,841.4	609.1	33.1
1973-74	1,674.6	463.1	27.7	193.6	131.0	67.7	1,868.2	594.1	31.8
1974-75	1,827.2	509.4	27.9	185.2	123.2	66.5	2,012.4	632.6	31.4
1975-76	1,900.3	522.4	27.5	204.2	140.2	68.7	2,104.5	662.6	31.5
1976-77	1,810.4	517.3	28.6	210.3	149.2	70.9	2,020.7	666.5	33.0
1977-78	1,915.7	473.9	24.7	216.2	149.3	69.1	2,131.9	623.2	29.2
1978-79	1,909.3	453.3	23.7	210.3	134.8	64.1	2,119.6	588.1	27.7
1979-80	2,181.9	590.3	27.1	228.2	146.4	63.6	2,410.1	736.7	30.6
1980-81	2,085.2	519.5	25.0	217.4	135.7	62.4	2,302.6	655.2	28.4
1981-82	2,002.6	383.1	19.1	223.3	140.8	63.0	2,225.9	523.9	23.5
1982-83	2,052.7	478.4	23.3	198.3	121.2	61.1	2,251.0	599.6	26.6
1983-84	2,050.2	362.0	17.7	182.2	107.2	58.8	2,232.6	469.2	21.0
1984-85	1,922.4	377.3	19.6	183.0	111.2	60.8	2,105.0	448.5	21.3

Source: Sunkist Growers, various issues.
[a] September 1 through August 31.
[b] Includes tangerines and tangelos.
[c] Four-fifths bushel carton.

Table 1.2. Orange bearing acreage and production, by states, 1957-58 through 1985-86.

Crop year[a]	FLORIDA Bearing acreage	FLORIDA Prod.	FLORIDA Yield	CALIFORNIA Bearing acreage	CALIFORNIA Prod.	CALIFORNIA Yield	TEXAS Bearing acreage	TEXAS Prod.	TEXAS Yield	ARIZONA Bearing acreage	ARIZONA Prod.	ARIZONA Yield	UNITED STATES Bearing acreage	UNITED STATES Prod.	UNITED STATES Yield
	1,000 acres	1,000 tons	tons/acre	1,000 acres	1,000 tons	tons/acres	1,000 acres	1,000 tons	tons/acres	1,000 acres	1,000 tons	tons/acres	1,000 acres	1,000 tons	tons/acres
1957-58	355.6	3,645	10.25	148.6	860	5.79	28.0	90	3.21	6.7	47	7.01	543.4	4,651	8.56
1958-59	353.4	3,735	10.57	145.0	1,493	10.30	30.0	103	3.43	6.6	23	3.48	539.5	5,364	9.94
1959-60	370.0	3,941	10.65	138.7	1,142	8.23	31.9	122	3.82	7.4	56	7.57	552.5	5,273	9.54
1960-61	374.1	3,721	9.95	136.5	926	6.78	35.0	158	4.51	7.7	44	5.71	557.8	4,861	8.71
1961-62	408.7	4,896	11.98	131.6	758	5.76	32.4	103	3.18	8.7	54	6.21	585.9	5,823	9.94
1962-63	370.0	3,262	8.82	127.9	1,061	8.30	35.0	2	.06	9.8	59	6.02	543.7	4,385	8.07
1963-64	388.0	2,469	6.36	127.7	1,151	9.01	26.0	11	.42	11.7	83	7.09	554.6	3,732	6.73
1964-65	435.0	3,708	8.52	122.4	1,151	9.40	26.0	40	1.54	13.8	91	6.59	598.4	4,990	8.34
1965-66	472.0	4,316	9.14	125.7	1,346	10.71	27.0	59	2.19	16.8	91	5.42	641.5	5,812	9.06
1966-67	522.0	6,276	12.02	130.4	1,380	10.58	29.0	122	4.21	23.5	147	6.26	704.9	7,925	11.24
1967-68	557.6	4,524	8.11	139.9	718	5.13	31.0	81	2.61	19.3	117	6.06	747.8	5,440	7.27
1968-69	595.6	5,836	9.80	150.5	1,661	11.04	35.0	203	5.80	19.3	202	10.47	800.4	7,902	9.87
1969-70	636.1	6,197	9.74	160.2	1,463	9.13	35.0	189	5.40	15.5	174	11.23	846.8	8,023	9.47
1970-71	660.5	6,402	9.69	167.9	1,406	8.37	40.5	263	6.49	18.1	134	7.40	887.0	8,205	9.25
1971-72	624.2	6,165	9.88	180.4	1,627	9.02	42.5	261	6.14	19.5	184	9.44	866.6	8,237	9.50
1972-73	619.6	7,636	12.32	188.8	1,579	8.36	35.0	332	9.49	24.5	190	7.76	867.9	9,737	11.22
1973-74	614.6	7,461	12.14	196.0	1,516	7.73	32.5	281	8.65	24.4	128	5.25	867.5	9,386	10.82
1974-75	610.4	7,799	12.78	196.9	2,063	10.48	30.9	193	6.25	24.1	186	7.72	862.3	10,241	11.88
1975-76	596.4	8,154	13.67	197.7	1,980	10.02	30.9	259	8.38	23.0	100	4.35	848.0	10,493	12.37
1976-77	594.3	8,406	14.14	192.5	1,699	8.83	28.2	293	10.39	21.0	148	7.05	836.0	10,546	12.61
1977-78	579.0	7,551	13.04	188.6	1,599	8.48	28.4	260	9.15	16.8	136	8.10	812.8	9,546	11.74
1978-79	571.5	7,380	12.91	187.1	1,399	7.48	27.8	272	9.78	14.8	109	7.36	801.2	9,160	11.43
1979-80	576.6	9,302	16.13	185.7	2,228	12.00	28.0	171	6.11	15.7	131	8.34	806.0	11,832	14.68
1980-81	573.4	7,758	13.53	182.7	2,447	13.39	25.3	184	7.27	13.2	98	7.42	794.6	10,487	13.20
1981-82	560.2	5,661	10.11	179.7	1,572	8.75	23.7	252	10.63	13.5	115	8.52	777.1	7,600	9.78
1982-83	536.8	6,282	11.70	177.4	2,854	16.09	24.0	241	10.04	12.6	142	11.27	750.8	9,519	12.68
1983-84	474.3	5,252	11.07	177.5	1,819	10.25	24.3	107	4.40	12.6	68	5.40	688.7	7,246	10.52
1984-85	420.1	4,676	11.13	175.2	1,966	11.22	11.4	0	0.00	10.9	92	8.44	617.6	6,734	10.32
1985-86[b]	367.6	5,355	11.57	174.7	2,057	11.77	11.4	13	1.14	10.9	87	7.98	564.6	7,512	13.30

Source: Florida Crop and Livestock Reporting Service, various issues.
[a]September 1 through August 31.
[b]Preliminary.

Table 1.3. Grapefruit bearing acreage and production, by states, 1957-58 through 1985-86.

Crop year[a]	FLORIDA			TEXAS			CALIFORNIA			ARIZONA			UNITED STATES		
	Bearing acreage	Prod.	Yield	Bearing acreage	Prod.	Yield	Bearing acreage	Prod.	Yield	Bearing acreage	Prod.	Yield	Bearing acreage	Prod.	Yield
	1,000 acres	1,000 tons	tons/ acres	1,000 acres	1,000 tons	tons/ acres	1,000 acres	1,000 tons	tons/ acres	1,000 acres	1,000 tons	tons/ acres	1,000 acres	1,000 tons	tons/ acres
1957-58	95.0	1,322	13.92	30.1	140	4.65	7.5	79	10.53	5.4	89	16.48	138.0	1,630	11.81
1958-59	94.0	1,496	15.91	34.1	168	4.93	7.4	84	11.35	5.6	60	10.71	141.1	1,808	12.81
1959-60	92.3	1,297	14.05	38.1	208	5.46	7.6	87	11.45	5.6	103	18.39	143.6	1,695	11.80
1960-61	92.5	1,343	14.52	40.0	272	6.80	8.1	86	10.62	5.7	75	13.16	146.3	1,776	12.14
1961-62	94.0	1,479	15.73	45.3	108	2.38	9.5	92	9.68	5.8	69	11.90	154.6	1,748	11.31
1962-63	88.0	1,275	14.49	35.0	3	.09	10.9	82	7.52	6.0	69	11.50	139.9	1,429	10.21
1963-64	83.0	1,117	13.46	36.0	20	.56	11.9	137	11.51	6.0	103	17.17	136.9	1,377	10.06
1964-65	84.0	1,356	16.14	36.0	80	2.22	12.3	138	11.22	6.1	93	15.25	138.4	1,667	12.04
1965-66	85.8	1,483	17.28	37.0	152	4.11	12.6	161	12.78	6.7	98	14.63	142.1	1,894	13.33
1966-67	87.0	1,854	21.31	39.0	216	5.54	12.8	162	12.66	6.9	54	7.83	145.7	2,286	15.69
1967-68	87.5	1,399	15.99	41.0	112	2.73	12.8	150	11.72	7.6	120	15.79	148.9	1,781	11.96
1968-69	90.3	1,697	18.79	45.0	268	5.56	12.7	164	12.91	4.9	80	16.33	152.9	2,209	14.45
1969-70	98.7	1,590	16.11	40.0	324	8.10	12.8	171	13.36	6.1	101	16.56	157.6	2,186	13.87
1970-71	107.2	1,824	17.01	37.6	404	10.74	12.1	164	13.55	6.3	81	12.86	163.2	2,473	15.15
1971-72	112.6	1,999	17.75	35.0	368	10.51	12.6	179	14.21	6.4	81	12.66	166.6	2,627	15.77
1972-73	114.6	1,930	16.84	35.0	472	13.49	13.1	189	14.43	8.0	85	10.63	170.7	2,676	15.67
1973-74	115.8	2,044	17.65	35.0	428	12.23	14.3	154	10.77	8.2	66	8.05	173.3	2,692	15.53
1974-75	115.4	1,897	16.44	33.1	292	8.82	15.8	226	14.30	9.3	89	9.57	173.6	2,504	14.42
1975-76	117.9	2,088	17.71	33.1	428	12.93	16.4	234	14.27	9.6	100	10.42	177.0	2,850	16.10
1976-77	119.3	2,190	18.36	35.1	496	14.13	16.6	250	15.06	10.2	96	9.41	181.2	3,032	16.73
1977-78	120.3	2,184	18.15	40.1	476	11.87	17.4	274	15.75	10.8	96	8.89	188.6	3,030	16.07
1978-79	124.6	2,125	17.05	39.8	360	9.05	19.5	200	10.26	8.9	72	8.09	192.8	2,757	14.30
1979-80	126.4	2,329	18.43	43.8	316	7.21	21.3	245	11.50	8.4	96	11.43	199.9	2,986	14.94
1980-81	125.6	2,138	17.02	41.5	268	6.46	21.8	263	12.06	8.1	90	11.11	197.0	2,759	14.00
1981-82	127.8	2,044	15.99	41.1	556	13.53	22.0	201	9.14	8.1	77	9.51	199.0	2,878	14.46
1982-83	128.6	1,674	13.02	42.2	448	10.62	21.7	238	10.97	6.8	87	12.79	193.3	2,447	12.28
1983-84	119.6	1,738	14.52	43.2	128	2.96	21.9	237	10.82	6.8	73	10.74	191.5	2,176	11.36
1984-85	115.5	1,870	16.19	19.1	0	0.00	21.1	289	13.70	7.1	96	13.52	162.8	2,255	13.85
1985-86[b]	105.1	1,987	18.91	19.1	.47	9.00	20.9	276	13.21	7.1	77	10.85	152.2	2,349	15.43

Source: Florida Crop and Livestock Reporting Service, various issues.
[a]September 1 through August 31.
[b]Preliminary.

Geographic Distribution. Florida, California, Texas, and Arizona are the four major citrus producing states in the United States. In 1985–86 Florida accounted for 65 percent of the orange bearing acreage and 71 percent of the production, while California had 23 percent of the orange bearing acreage and supplied 27 percent of the production. Texas acreage was approximately equal to that of Arizona; however, Arizona production was 6.7 times that of Texas (Table 1.2). Regional shifts in orange bearing acreage are slight but show Texas and Arizona decreasing in acreage share from 7.4 percent in 1966–67 to 3.9 percent in 1985–86. Annual regional production shares fluctuate, depending on regional differences in weather and production conditions; however, the production shares of Texas and Arizona have fallen from 5.4 percent in 1971–72 to 1.3 percent in 1985–86. The production shares between Florida and California have increased for California in the 1980s due to the numerous freezes in Florida that have decreased acreage and yields.

Florida is also the major supplier of grapefruit, with 69 percent of the acreage and 85 percent of the production in 1985–86. In contrast to the orange production, Texas produced the second largest grapefruit supply totaling 19 percent of the market, while California supplied 7 percent in 1981–82 (Table 1.3). In 1985–86 Texas production was almost zero because of the freezes. In addition to production differences Florida has consistently shown a higher yield per acre for both oranges and grapefruit. From the 1974–75 season through 1978–79, Florida's yield exceeded the average of the remaining states by 33 percent for oranges and 33 percent for grapefruit. From 1979–80 through 1985–86 Florida's yield exceeded California's by only 2.4 percent for oranges and 40.2 percent for grapefruit.

Finally differences in the acreage of bearing versus nonbearing fruit trees provide an indication of the short-run growth that can be expected within each region. In 1969 approximately 11 percent of Florida's orange acreage was represented by young, nonbearing acreage, while over 27 percent of the California-Arizona acreage was nonbearing. By 1975 Florida's nonbearing acreage declined to 32,135 acres or 5 percent of the total. The California-Arizona nonbearing acreage declined to 6 percent by 1975 leaving 14,918 acres nonbearing. Since 1975 Florida's nonbearing acreage has increased from 32,135 to 98,671 acres while California's nonbearing acreage has declined from 14,918 to 4,334 acres (Table 1.4). Most of Florida's increases in plantings are attributed to replanting after freezes. Even with the increase in plantings, Florida's total acreage was 35 percent lower in 1986 than in 1969 when Florida's acreage was 715,806 acres. If the decline in new plantings in California continues, any increase in production will depend upon increases in the yields of bearing trees as the trees mature in age.

8

Table 1.4. Florida and California-Arizona total and nonbearing orange acreage, 1969 through 1986.

Year	FLORIDA[a] Total acreage	Nonbearing acreage	Percentage of total acreage	CALIFORNIA-ARIZONA[b] Total acreage	Nonbearing acreage	Percentage of total acreage
1969	715,806	79,687	11	249,979	66,933	27
1971	659,418	35,209	5	247,389	54,846	22
1973	624,431	27,823	4	249,444	36,551	15
1975	628,567	32,135	5	233,667	14,918	6
1976	628,567	32,135	5	221,496	8,577	4
1978	616,020	37,052	6	206,500	4,627	2
1980	627,174	50,559	8	200,311	4,378	2
1982	636,864	76,661	12	194,042	4,020	2
1984	573,991	99,722	17	190,675	4,334	2
1986	466,252	98,671	NA	NA	NA	NA

Source: [a]Florida Citrus Mutual, various issues.
[b]Sunkist Growers, various issues.
NA = not available.

Production and Consumption of Products Derived from Citrus

Citrus is consumed either as fresh fruit or as some form of processed product. The utilization depends on the type of citrus, variety, geographical production region, and consumer preferences. Processing citrus also generates a number of by-products used as food additives, cattle feeds, cosmetics, medicines, and so forth. In contrast, fresh packing does not generate by-products. Rather, citrus from packinghouses that is of unacceptable quality (i.e., eliminations) is diverted into processed products.

Prior to the early fifties most citrus was consumed in a fresh form. Processing technologies developed and implemented in the fifties led to a major change in the forms of citrus consumption. Today most processed citrus is marketed as frozen concentrated orange juice, canned single strength juice, and chilled single strength juice. The development of processing technology has been the most significant factor leading to structural change within the citrus industry.

Fresh Citrus Consumption. Approximately 27 percent of the U.S. orange crop is consumed as fresh fruit. This percentage is equal to the 1966–67 season, continued to trend slightly downward during the late 1960s and the 1970s, and increased during the early 1980s to 31 percent for the 1984–85 season (Table 1.5). The differences in utilization of oranges for fresh or processed products among producing regions form one of the reasons for significant differences in the marketing structure of the producing states. In 1984–85 California-Arizona marketed 78 percent of their oranges in fresh form and 56 percent of Texas oranges in 1983–84 was sold fresh. Florida's share marketed as fresh fruit has trended downward since the 1967–68 season (Table 1.5). California-Arizona remains the largest supplier of fresh oranges with 80 percent of the market, while Florida accounts for 16 percent and Texas 4 percent.

Table 1.5. Production and utilization of oranges by states, 1966-67 through 1984-85.

Crop year[a]	CALIFORNIA-ARIZONA Total	Fresh	Fresh %	FLORIDA Total	Fresh	Fresh %	TEXAS Total	Fresh	Fresh %	TOTAL U.S. Total	Fresh	Fresh %
	Mil. cartons[b]		%	Mil. cartons[b]		%	Mil. cartons[b]		%	Mil. cartons[b]		%
1966-67	82.6	58.4	71	279.0	35.8	17	5.6	3.7	66	367.2	97.9	27
1967-68	44.5	27.5	64	201.0	34.2	17	3.6	3.0	83	249.1	65.8	26
1968-69	99.4	59.5	60	259.4	26.6	10	9.0	4.3	48	367.8	90.4	25
1969-70	87.3	57.8	66	275.4	26.5	10	8.4	4.8	57	371.1	89.1	24
1970-71	82.1	54.1	66	284.6	27.9	10	12.4	6.3	51	379.1	88.3	23
1971-72	96.6	58.9	61	274.0	22.5	8	12.3	5.5	45	382.9	86.9	23
1972-73	94.3	53.9	57	339.4	24.4	7	15.6	6.4	41	449.3	84.7	19
1973-74	87.6	62.8	72	331.6	22.2	7	13.2	4.8	36	432.4	89.8	21
1974-75	119.9	77.1	64	346.6	26.8	8	9.1	4.8	53	475.6	108.7	23
1975-76	111.0	70.9	64	362.4	23.5	6	12.2	6.2	51	485.6	100.6	21
1976-77	98.5	69.8	71	373.6	17.8	5	13.8	6.8	49	485.9	94.4	19
1977-78	92.4	62.9	68	335.6	19.9	6	12.2	6.3	52	440.2	89.1	20
1978-79	80.4	52.8	66	328.0	23.4	7	12.8	4.2	33	421.2	80.4	19
1979-80	125.8	83.4	66	413.4	22.0	5	8.1	4.2	52	547.3	109.6	20
1980-81	135.7	78.6	58	344.8	16.6	5	8.7	5.7	66	489.2	100.9	21
1981-82	89.9	71.0	79	251.6	15.2	6	11.9	6.6	55	353.4	92.8	26
1982-83	159.8	91.6	57	279.2	20.6	7	11.4	6.7	59	450.4	118.9	26
1983-84	100.6	78.1	78	231.4	15.3	7	5.0	2.8	56	337.0	96.2	29
1984-85	108.9	85.2	78	207.8	13.3	6	c	c	c	316.7	98.5	31

Source: Sunkist Growers, various issues.
[a]September 1 through August 31.
[b]Four-fifths bushel carton.
[c]Due to Dec. 1983 freeze no commercial supplies were harvested.

Grapefruit consumption differs from orange consumption in that approximately 44 percent of the grapefruit crop is consumed fresh. This share has varied somewhat over the last five years (Table 1.6). Florida provides about 62 percent of the U.S. fresh grapefruit supply, and approximately 38 percent of Florida's production is sold fresh. Texas and California have 17 and 23 percent of the fresh grapefruit market with 58 percent of the Texas crop going fresh and 55 percent of California's crop sold in fresh form (Table 1.6).

Considerable regional competition exists in the fresh citrus markets. This is especially significant since the U.S. per capita consumption of fresh oranges has slowly trended downward since 1967 and grapefruit

Table 1.6. Production and utilization of grapefruit by states, 1964-65 through 1984-85.

Crop year[a]	CALIFORNIA-ARIZONA			FLORIDA			TEXAS			TOTAL U.S.		
	Total	Fresh	Fresh	Total	Fresh	Fresh	Total	Fresh	Fresh	Total	Fresh	Fresh
	Mil. cartons[b]		%	Mil. cartons[b]		%	Mil. cartons[b]		%	Mil. cartons[b]		%
1964-65	14.3	8.8	62	63.8	31.7	50	4.0	3.7	93	82.1	44.2	54
1965-66	15.8	9.7	61	69.8	30.1	43	7.6	6.2	82	93.2	46.0	49
1966-67	13.4	7.8	58	87.2	34.6	40	11.2	8.1	72	111.8	50.5	45
1967-68	16.7	10.5	63	65.8	29.4	45	5.6	4.6	82	88.1	44.5	51
1968-69	15.1	8.0	53	79.8	28.1	35	13.4	9.2	69	108.3	45.3	42
1969-70	16.8	9.0	54	74.8	28.5	38	16.2	9.9	61	107.8	47.4	44
1970-71	15.1	7.0	46	85.8	29.9	35	20.2	11.9	59	121.1	48.8	40
1971-72	15.9	8.3	52	94.0	34.1	36	18.4	11.5	63	128.3	53.9	42
1972-73	16.9	8.1	48	90.8	34.1	38	23.6	12.7	54	131.3	54.9	42
1973-74	13.4	7.1	53	96.2	37.5	39	21.4	10.8	50	131.0	55.4	42
1974-75	19.4	9.9	51	89.2	37.6	42	14.6	9.3	64	123.2	56.8	46
1975-76	20.6	9.8	48	98.2	40.7	41	21.4	14.5	68	140.2	65.0	46
1976-77	21.4	11.4	53	103.0	32.8	32	24.8	13.0	52	149.2	57.2	38
1977-78	22.7	11.3	50	102.8	36.1	35	23.8	13.2	55	149.3	60.6	41
1978-79	16.8	9.5	57	100.0	39.6	40	18.0	8.0	44	134.8	57.1	42
1979-80	21.0	9.6	46	109.6	39.0	36	15.8	8.4	53	146.4	57.0	39
1980-81	21.7	12.2	56	100.6	34.3	34	13.4	9.3	69	135.7	55.8	41
1981-82	17.1	9.6	56	96.2	33.4	35	27.8	14.5	52	141.1	57.5	41
1982-83	20.0	12.1	61	78.8	36.6	46	22.4	15.6	70	121.2	64.3	53
1983-84	19.0	12.3	65	81.8	33.3	41	6.4	5.7	89	100.8	51.3	51
1984-85	23.2	16.3	70	88.8	30.0	34	c	c	c	112.0	46.3	41

Source: Sunkist Growers, various issues.
[a]September 1 through August 31.
[b]Four-fifths bushel carton.
[c]Due to Dec. 1983 freeze no commercial supplies were harvested.

has trended downward since 1976 (Table 1.7). Growth in the consumption of regional supplies occurs as a result of increases in population, redistribution of shares among regions, and development of foreign markets. The latter two alternatives suggest a degree of competition among the supplying regions.

Utilization and Consumption of Oranges and Grapefruit. The processing share of the citrus industry differs substantially among the regions. Florida processed 89 percent of the citrus (oranges and grapefruit) grown in the United States in 1984–85 (Tables 1.5 and 1.6). This figure is broken down among individual products as 98 percent of the frozen concentrated orange and grapefruit juice, 80 percent of the canned orange juice, and 76 percent of the canned grapefruit juice. Bulk juice packs will ultimately be reprocessed into retail and/or institutional packs or used for manufacturing.

Since Florida is the major domestic supplier of processed citrus, the relative distribution of production of processed products in Florida pro-

Table 1.7. United States per capita consumption of fresh citrus,
1966 through 1984.

Year	Oranges	Grapefruit	Total citrus
		Pounds	
1966	16.4	8.4	29.1
1967	18.0	9.0	31.6
1968	14.1	8.0	26.2
1969	16.3	7.8	28.2
1970	16.3	8.2	28.6
1971	16.1	8.6	29.2
1972	14.6	8.6	27.2
1973	14.4	8.6	27.4
1974	14.4	8.2	27.4
1975	15.9	8.4	29.4
1976	14.7	9.2	29.0
1977	13.4	7.7	26.2
1978	13.5	8.3	26.5
1979	12.4	7.6	24.5
1980	15.8	8.0	28.9
1981	13.5	6.9	25.0
1982	12.7	7.5	24.7
1983	15.5	8.1	28.7
1984	12.8	6.1	23.7

Source: Sunkist Growers, various issues.

vides a profile of the U.S. processing sector. Approximately 79 percent
of all Florida oranges is processed into frozen concentrated orange juice.
This percentage will vary from season to season depending on crop conditions. In contrast, approximately 2 percent of the oranges is processed
into canned single strength juices, while approximately 13 percent is
marketed as chilled orange juice. The remaining 6 percent is sold in fresh
form (Table 1.8). Grapefruit concentrate accounts for 45 percent of the
Florida supply, canned grapefruit totaled 11 percent, and chilled grapefruit accounted for 4 percent of the Florida grapefruit crop. The remaining 40 percent goes for fresh use (Table 1.9). Each processed product
may be marketed in retail and/or institutional packs or in bulk form in
the case of concentrate. Furthermore, concentrate can be reconstituted
and sold at retail as chilled juice. Thus, the percentages of product form
at retail are likely different from the figures given at the processor level.
(Chapter 9 discusses the important role of imports of orange juice into
the United States.)

Annual per capita consumption of frozen orange concentrate increased from 1.84 single strength gallons in 1972 to 2.41 single strength
gallons in 1976 (Table 1.10). Since 1976 the trend has been mixed with a
low of 1.34 single strength gallons in 1979 and has never returned to the
1976 level. Chilled orange juice has increased consistently since 1972

Table 1.8. Florida processing plant and packinghouse orange utilization by product from 1975-76 through 1985-86.

Products	VOLUME OF ORANGES										
	1975-76	1976-77	1977-78	1978-79	1979-80	1980-81	1981-82	1982-83	1983-84	1984-85	1985-86
	Thousands of 1 3/5 bushel boxes										
Fresh, interstate, & intrastate	11,811	8,510	10,492	11,800	12,194	7,870	7,125	10,326	6,866	4,219	9,417
Exports	841	190	238	557	186	158	89	166	42	1	101
Noncertified, gift fruit, & roadside sales	1,423	1,363	1,287	1,514	1,441	1,382	1,278	1,397	1,544	199	358
Total fresh	14,075	10,063	12,017	13,871	13,821	9,410	8,492	11,889	8,452	4,419	9,876
Percentage	7.4%	5.2%	6.8%	8%	6.3%	5.2%	6.4%	8.1%	6.9%	4.1%	8.1%
Cannery juice	6,308	7,429	7,210	6,163	6,656	5,994	4,058	2,190	2,269	1,039	1,292
Cannery blend	526	473	523	348	409	336	208	140	102	91	69
Cannery sections & salad	56	35	51	35	33	39	31	68	NA	NA	NA
Total cannery	6,890	7,937	7,784	6,546	7,098	6,369	4,297	2,398	2,371	1,130	1,361
Percentage	3.6%	4.1%	4.4%	3.8%	3.3%	3.6%	3.2%	1.7%	2.0%	1.1%	1.1%
Frozen concentrate (boxes)	144,526	147,771	130,929	129,123	173,229	144,322	104,355	114,343	94,016	86,112	96,061
Total concentrate (boxes)	144,526	147,771	130,929	129,123	173,229	144,322	104,355	114,343	94,016	86,112	96,061
Percentage	76.0%	76.4%	74.2%	74.8%	79.1%	80.2%	78.0%	77.8%	77.2%	80.8%	78.7%
Chilled juice	24,005	27,250	25,408	22,793	24,430	19,640	16,293	18,084	16,980	14,903	14,732
Chilled sections & salad	608	528	621	378	383	315	309	227	NA	NA	NA
Total chilled	24,626	27,628	25,791	23,108	24,739	19,867	16,518	18,254	16,980	14,903	14,732
Percentage	13.0%	14.3%	14.6%	13.4%	11.3%	11.0%	12.4%	12.4%	13.9%	14.0%	12.1%
Total utilization	190,117	193,399	176,521	172,648	218,887	179,968	133,662	146,884	121,819	106,564	122,030

Source: Florida Citrus Mutual, various issues.
Note: Crop year is September 1 through August 31.
NA = not available.

Table 1.9. Florida processing plant and packinghouse grapefruit utilization by product from 1975-76 through 1985-86.

Products	1975-76	1976-77	1977-78	1978-79	1979-80	1980-81	1981-82	1982-83	1983-84	1984-85	1985-86
					VOLUME OF GRAPEFRUIT						
				Thousands of 1 3/5 bushel boxes							
Fresh, interstate, & intrastate	15,289	11,224	13,713	13,462	13,361	10,953	10,882	12,546	10,849	11,941	13,821
Exports	4,101	4,259	3,303	5,265	4,987	5,120	4,967	4,762	4,976	2,833	5,539
Other uses[a]	996	910	1,033	1,068	1,158	1,093	962	1,064	915	235	260
Total fresh	20,386	16,393	18,049	19,795	19,506	17,166	16,811	18,372	16,740	15,009	19,620
Percentage	41.8%	32.2%	35.0%	39.5%	35.6%	34.1%	34.9%	46.7%	41.8%	35.1%	43.1%
Cannery juice	12,545	14,359	12,144	11,160	10,520	8,493	7,708	3,938	3,134	3,614	3,036
Cannery sections	1,229	1,276	1,339	1,388	1,463	1,262	981	1,129	0	0	0
Cannery blend	590	538	630	449	445	348	229	171	117	111	88
Cannery salad	46	44	60	40	33	36	37	53	0	0	0
Total cannery	14,410	16,217	14,173	13,037	12,461	10,139	8,955	5,291	3,251	3,725	3,124
Percentage	29.6%	31.9%	27.5%	26.1%	22.7%	20.2%	18.6%	13.4%	8.1%	8.7%	6.9%
Frozen concentrate	8,986	13,020	13,998	13,276	18,506	19,489	20,052	13,977	18,728	22,996	21,572
Frozen blend	1	0	1	0	0	1	0	0	0	0	0
Total concentrate	8,987	13,020	13,999	13,276	18,506	19,490	20,052	13,977	18,728	22,996	21,572
Percentage	18.4%	25.6%	27.2%	26.5%	33.7%	38.8%	41.7%	35.5%	46.8%	53.7%	47.4%
Chilled juice	3,920	4,330	4,375	3,162	3,592	2,847	1,697	1,314	1,320	1,065	1,189
Chilled sections	441	535	407	402	475	436	368	222	0	0	0
Chilled salad	613	400	510	369	325	206	261	195	0	0	0
Total chilled	4,974	5,265	5,292	3,933	4,392	3,489	2,326	1,731	1,320	1,065	1,189
Percentage	10.2%	10.3%	10.3%	7.9%	8.0%	6.9%	4.8%	4.4%	3.3%	2.5%	2.6%
Total utilization	48,757	50,895	51,513	50,041	54,865	50,284	48,144	39,371	40,039	42,795	45,145

Source: Florida Citrus Mutual, various issues.
Note: Crop year is September 1 through August 31.
[a]Noncertified gift fruit and roadside sales.

13

Table 1.10. Per capita retail consumption of processed oranges, 1972 through 1986.

Year	Population[a]	Frozen concentrated orange juice[b]	Chilled orange juice[b]	Canned single strength orange juice[b]
	Thousands	Single strength equivalent gallons		
1972	208,800	1.84	.32	.034
1973	210,400	2.00	.39	.031
1974	211,900	2.20	.41	.030
1975	213,540	2.39	.48	.029
1976	215,120	2.41	.53	.027
1977	216,700	2.23	.58	.029
1978	217,440	1.95	.60	.104
1979	219,340	1.34[c]	.47[c]	.060[c]
1980	223,670	1.57	.68	.091
1981	228,350	2.27	.68	.077
1982	230,700	2.17	.69	.063
1983	232,900	2.02	.78	.057
1984	233,991	1.95	.96	.045
1985	236,697	1.24	.65	.030
1986[d]	239,224	1.25	.79	.022

Source: [a]Nielsen Marketing Service.
[b]Florida Department of Citrus, Economic and Market Research Department, various issues.
[c]Data available for nine months only (December 1978–August 1979).
[d]Stopped reporting in July 1986.

with the exception of 1979, 1985, and 1986. The consumption of canned orange juice has been mixed over this same time period but has shown a downward trend since 1980 (Table 1.10).

Most of the data on retail consumption are available through commercial data sources including Market Research Corporation of America, A. C. Nielsen Co., and NPD Group Marketing and Research Companies. These data apply to U.S. domestic consumption for both domestic and imported juice. Institutional consumption data are generally less detailed and often unavailable for certain products.

2

●
●
●
●
Structure
of the
Domestic Industry

●
●
●
●
●
●
●
●
●
●
●

Number of Firms and Ownership

General statistics on the number of firms at each stage of production and marketing are given in Table 2.1. The *1982 Census of Agriculture* shows Florida with 8,169 growers, California with 5,365 growers, Arizona with 452 growers, and Texas with 1,139. The packing and processing sector in Florida is slightly larger than California-Arizona and Texas.

Almost all fresh citrus consumed is from domestic sources. In contrast, nearly half of the processed juices is, in recent years, packaged from imported orange concentrate. The statistics reported for the domestic processing industry must be interpreted recognizing the significant impact that imports have on the overall industry structure. Large

Table 2.1. Number of packinghouses, processing firms, and grove producers by state.

	Florida	California-Arizona	Texas
Growers[a]	8,169	5,817	1,139
Packinghouses	157[b]	136[c]	23[d]
Processors	85[b]	3[c]	2[e]

Source: [a]U.S. Department of Commerce, Bureau of Census (a).
[b]Division of Fruit and Vegetable Inspection, 1983-84.
[c]Mueller et al. (1987: 40, 43, 97). 1979-80 information.
[d]Edwards and Camp (1987). 1982-83 information.
[e]Industry sources.

dairy distributors and recon-operators have gained an increasing share of the consumer market as they reprocess imported concentrate into ready-to-serve juices. The growth of this phase of processing with much of it occurring outside of Florida has had a profound impact on the total U.S. processing competitive structure.

Packinghouse and Processing Firms. Within the Florida industry there were 157 registered fresh fruit packers (Table 2.2) and 85 processors (Table 2.1) in 1983–84. These firms varied in size, and in some seasons were totally inactive. Approximately 25 percent of the fresh volume was sold by packers under a cooperative structure, and both

Table 2.2. Total and average annual Florida citrus packinghouse shipments and plant numbers from 1952-53 through 1983-84.

Season[a]	Total packinghouse shipments (1 3/5 bushel equivalent)	Average annual packinghouse shipments (1 3/5 bushel equivalent)	Number of packinghouses
1952-53	41,270,062	149,529	276
1953-54	46,081,412	168,180	274
1954-55	43,012,776	164,170	262
1955-56	41,619,749	172,696	241
1956-57	38,475,959	174,890	220
1957-58	29,309,212	140,909	208
1958-59	28,332,040	160,977	176
1959-60	31,469,424	173,864	181
1960-61	28,310,435	159,047	178
1961-62	34,783,396	205,818	169
1962-63	22,484,665	118,340	190
1963-64	23,697,756	145,385	163
1964-65	27,999,170	174,994	160
1965-66	28,681,718	127,474	225
1966-67	34,380,175	185,838	185
1967-68	30,006,290	170,490	176
1968-69	25,813,484	152,742	169
1969-70	27,567,531	130,651	211
1970-71	29,332,061	156,021	188
1971-72	30,099,804	183,535	164
1972-73	32,067,325	195,532	164
1973-74	32,452,362	200,323	162
1974-75	35,931,432	225,983	159
1975-76	37,879,098	224,136	169
1976-77	29,245,210	169,047	173
1977-78	32,471,416	216,476	150
1978-79	35,930,170	242,771	148
1979-80	36,439,588	241,322	151
1980-81	28,612,028	197,324	145
1981-82	26,712,076	179,276	149
1982-83	31,730,555	212,957	149
1983-84	26,332,547	167,723	157

Source: Division of Fruit and Vegetable Inspection, various issues.
[a]August 1 through July 31.

private and cooperative packers sold approximately 40 percent of their fresh fruit through the central exchange, Sealdsweet.

The number of fresh fruit handlers in California was estimated to be 136 packinghouse firms in 1979–80. Of these an estimated 73 were affiliated with Sunkist (Mueller et al. 1987). While each handler competes for sales, the bulk of all functions is coordinated by Sunkist Growers Cooperative. Each of the Sunkist packing units is autonomous and each delegates its marketing responsibility to the district exchanges.

Virtually all of the Texas fresh citrus sold in commercial channels is handled in some 23 packinghouses. Four packers accounted for around 41 percent of all fresh shipments (Edwards and Camp 1987). The industry's processing is completed by two processors. The fresh industry is characterized as independent, individualistic, and highly competitive.

Integration. The extent of vertical integration is not fully known within any of the producing regions. However, the general pattern of vertical ownership can be identified. Within the California system historically a major share of citrus was sold under a cooperative arrangement via Sunkist Growers. Recent private acquisitions have led to a decline in the cooperative's share of the total California citrus crop. Cooperatives account for approximately 22 percent of the Florida processing volume. Vertical integration other than through cooperatives has been forward and backward. While data are sketchy, a reasonable estimate would be that around 10 percent of Florida's processing capacity is owned by vertically integrated family operations that hold substantial citrus acreage. Integration from the processor back to large citrus holdings is also present, but figures are not available. Many private processing organizations own some groves, but few are able to supply a large portion of their fruit need.

Rather than vertical integration, a more significant ownership arrangement among Florida processors is conglomerate integration. Of the total fruit processed an estimated 35 to 45 percent is processed by large firms that are subsidiaries of national food conglomerates (e.g., Coca-Cola). The influence of these large conglomerates on firm marketing strategies is readily apparent, especially in the areas of advertising and promotion.

Finally, within each producing region there is a large number of absentee owners. Many of these owners have simply invested in citrus land, speculating on inflating land values. These owners provide only minimal input into production decisions and usually contract for all production services.

Structure of Buyers and Sellers

Much of the discussion up to this point clearly shows the differences in product uses and structure of the industry among competing producing regions. The California industry is dominated by Sunkist marketing policies, while Texas firms are highly independent, with each setting most of its own marketing policies. Since Florida is the major producer of citrus and accounts for the largest share of all domestically processed products, many of the structural characteristics identified in this section will relate to structures of Florida. Discussions of the retail buyer side will relate to all citrus, however.

Relevant Markets. For the fresh market, the bulk of all fresh sales is through the commercial channels, with most of the fruit being distributed by the large retail chains. However, export markets have increased in importance as an alternative market. In 1976–77, 22.3 percent of the oranges and 25.6 percent of the U.S. grapefruit were exported. In 1985–86, 5.9 percent of the U.S. oranges was exported and 12.8 percent of the grapefruit was exported. The decrease in exports is due to the freezes in the United States (Florida Crop and Livestock Reporting Service). Sunkist coordinates most of the California-Arizona exports while Sealdsweet (Florida central exchange cooperative) is one of the major exporters in Florida. Most of these exports are completed with direct connections between these selling organizations and large foreign importers and trading companies.

On the processing side of the citrus industry the more important markets include retail outlets such as large chains, schools and institutions including restaurants, export markets, and manufacturing markets. Of these, the large retail chains play a dominant role with buyer power. The linkage between processors and retail chains is the most important marketing stage once citrus has been processed.

Retail Buyer Concentration. As suggested above, retail chains and large independents are the major buyers of both fresh and processed citrus. In 1986 large retail chains (over $100 million in sales) accounted for 79.6 percent of all retail food expenditures, while 16.8 percent of retail food expenditures was through large independents. The remaining retail outlets share totaled 3.6 percent. Similarly, nearly 97 percent of all retail orange concentrate moved through large retail food outlets, with chains accounting for 76 percent (Table 2.3). Percentages for other orange juices were slightly lower.

Table 2.3. Retail sales of frozen concentrated orange juice, 1986.

Store size	Market share	Share of orange concentrate sales	Share of other orange juices
Chains over $1 mil.	79.6%	75.8%	71.0%
Independents over $1 mil.	16.8	20.8	18.7
Chains under $1 mil.	0.9	0.3	4.2
Independents under $1 mil.	2.7	3.1	6.1

Source: Nielsen Marketing Service.

Figure 2.1 shows the downward trend in retail sales of frozen orange concentrate over the time period 1979 to 1985. This apparent downward trend is primarily due to a reduction in Florida's citrus supplies due to the freezes. A large share of Florida's citrus goes into the production of frozen concentrated orange juice (FCOJ) while only a small portion of FCOJ imports is used in the retail packs of FCOJ.

Figure 2.1. Frozen concentrated orange juice sales through retail outlets. *(From Nielsen Marketing Service)*

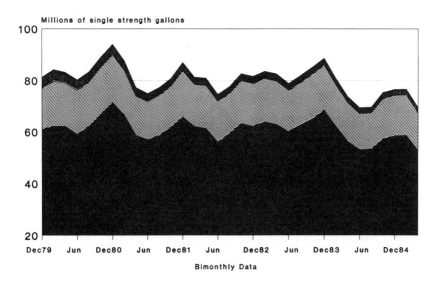

Packinghouse Concentration. Sunkist is the major seller for California and Arizona citrus, both fresh and processed. While the internal structure of the organization has changed, there is little evidence of any significant change in the market shares among California sellers. Also, the industry is highly concentrated, since Sunkist accounts for most of the state's supply.

Florida's fresh packers are generally more independent and competitive than California's fresh packers. Also, the Florida industry is highly competitive within the two major producing districts, the Indian River and interior regions. The concentration statistics for both regions are calculated based on the percentage of seasonal shipments accounted for by the largest firms in each district (Table 2.4). This has occurred

Table 2.4 Changes in the market share of the largest packinghouses within the Indian River and interior Florida districts, 1950-51 through 1983-84.

| Seasons | Percentage of fresh packed by a | | | |
	Largest packer	Four largest packers	Eight largest packers	Twenty largest packers
INDIAN RIVER				
1950-51[b]	13.63	45.56	66.35	97.04
1955-56[b]	15.90	41.77	61.85	90.17
1960-61[b]	17.61	41.00	61.67	94.12
1965-66[b]	12.44	33.25	51.86	91.39
1970-71[c]	10.06	26.91	45.83	81.38
1975-76[a]	5.02	19.57	37.19	73.59
1980-81[c]	6.36	23.03	40.97	74.18
1983-84[c]	6.23	24.44	43.00	76.40
INTERIOR FLORIDA				
1950-51[b]	4.93	16.85	26.07	46.02
1955-56[b]	7.44	23.28	32.94	55.22
1960-61[b]	9.87	28.34	43.20	67.40
1965-66[b]	10.22	28.74	43.64	65.70
1970-71[c]	5.81	17.73	30.08	55.77
1975-76[c]	6.90	21.72	36.56	65.34
1980-81[c]	9.91	23.56	38.23	67.87
1983-84[c]	11.27	28.84	47.19	75.18

[a]Each value is expressed as a percentage of the district's seasonal shipments.
[b]Ward and Smoleny (1973).
[c]Division of Fruit and Vegetable Inspection.

among the largest, 4 largest, 8 largest, and 20 largest firms. Total shipment volume has increased, and the entry of new firms and redistribution of firm sizes has led to decreases in Indian River firm concentration from 1950–51 through 1975–76. For example, the 8 largest firms' market decreased from 66 to 37 percent during this period. However, after this period the concentration among Indian River firms has shown a slight increase. Similar concentration statistics are calculated for the interior district, which has had increasing concentration (Table 2.4). However, the concentration in both districts is low.

Processor Concentration. Since Florida processors contribute 98 percent of the domestically produced frozen concentrated orange and grapefruit juices and 80 and 79 percent, respectively, of the canned orange and grapefruit juice for the United States, concentration statistics for only Florida processors are presented. The market shares of Florida citrus processors are first calculated according to the equivalent cases of single strength juices that a firm processes. Starting with the firm with the largest market share and adding the shares of the next largest firms in succession produces the accumulated market shares (Figure 2.2).

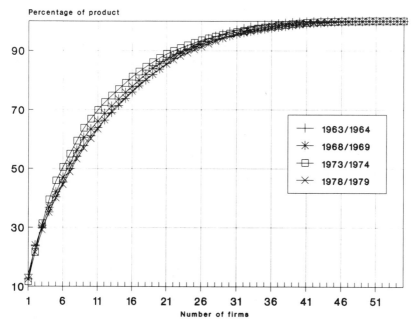

Figure 2.2. Accumulated market shares by Florida citrus processors.

These market shares are based on Florida production and, hence, do not include imports into the United States through non-Florida ports. The bottom axis ranks the firms, beginning with the largest. Accumulated market share curves are shown for the 1963–64, 1968–69, 1973–74, and 1978–79 seasons.

As will be discussed fully in Chapter 9, imports are primarily used to produced chilled ready-to-serve orange juice. Only minimal amounts of the imports outside of Florida go into the production of retail concentrate. Hence, the structural statistics for Florida concentrate processors represent a more accurate view of the competitive structure. However, looking only at the Florida data on chilled juice can be misleading. These two markets are highly interrelated and loss of market power in one juice market affects the entire domestic processing industry.

The accumulation curve shows that the largest processor has consistently maintained a market share in the vicinity of 12 percent. The combined shares of the four largest firms ranges from 35 to 40 percent. The relative closeness of the four accumulation curves, measured from the share of processed output per firm, indicates that only minor structural changes have taken place among the processing firms. However, the changes noted by the small difference in the curves suggest a slight movement toward greater concentration from 1963–64 to 1973–74 seasons; however, concentration drops again by 1978–79.

The amount of output attributable to a given percentage of the industry provides another measure of industry concentration. Figure 2.3 charts the cumulative percentages of output accounted for by percentage of firms. This relationship is known as a Lorenz curve and depicts the percentage of the industry output produced by a given percentage of the processors.

In 1973–74, 11 percent of the industry produced 50 percent of the output; however, in 1978–79, that percentage had dropped to 44 percent. Similarly, 50 percent of the processors accounted for over 90 percent of the output of the processed citrus industry in both seasons. The relative closeness of the curves further indicates that little change in firm concentration occurred.

The cumulative percentage of product in Figures 2.2 and 2.3 represents the market share of product produced but not the market share among selling organizations. An observed change in the structure of the Florida citrus processing industry has its origin in the development of a federated cooperative acting as the centralized sales agency for the output of its processing members. Instead of each processor marketing products individually and maintaining a sales force, one organization

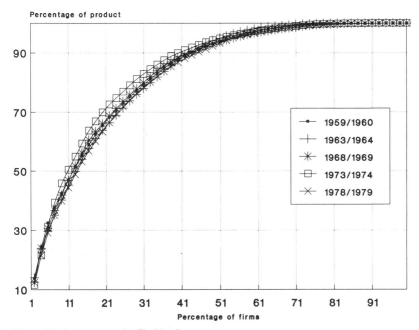

Figure 2.3. Lorenz curve for Florida citrus processors.

handles the sales function for all member firms. Thus, the concentration among selling firms is higher than among producing firms.

The benefits associated with the centralized sales effort are of two types. First, operational efficiencies result from a larger volume operation. Inputs such as materials can be procured at lower costs. Size also justifies expanded information processing facilities and computer applications. Second, by reducing the number of competing firms and offering a larger volume, a greater influence on price would be expected.

In addition to the results from the above figures, the distribution of firm sizes and the number of firms were used to derive a one-dimensional index of the citrus industry concentration. Values for the Herfindahl (HI), Hall-Tideman (HT), and Comprehensive Concentration (CCI) indices are shown in Table 2.5. Each index portrays a similar pattern of industry concentration for the 20 seasons since 1959–60. First, all indices indicate that the Florida citrus processing industry is not highly concentrated. This is evident from the small values of the Herfindahl and Hall-Tideman indices and the slightly higher value for the Comprehensive Concentration Index. Second, the values of each index show a high degree of stability over the periods studied, as measured by the coefficient of variation at the bottom of Table 2.5. The stability factor indicates that there has been little change in the market power accruing to specific citrus processing firms as a result of redistribution of market shares. Also, the entry and/or exit of firms, measured by firm numbers, has had little influence in initiating changes in the level of industry concentration.

The lowest values of the concentration indices shown in Table 2.5 are the values for $1/n$ for each season. This represents the hypothetical case of equal size distribution among firms within each production season. The calculated values HI and HT show only small deviations from this lower value. This deviation is considered small, since both HI and HT can deviate from $1/n$ by as much a $1-1/n$. The relatively small divergence of HI or HT from $1/n$ indicates that even though firm size dispersion exists, it does not greatly increase the industry concentration level above that measured by firm numbers alone. The CCI reflects similar patterns of low concentration over time, and the absolute magni-

Table 2.5.   Concentration indices for all Florida citrus processors, 1959-60 through 1978-79.

Seasons	$\frac{1}{n}$	Herfindahl Index (HI)	Hall-Tideman Index (HT)	Comprehensive Index (CCI)
1959-60	.0213	.0565	.0515	.2103
1960-61	.0213	.0592	.0532	.2204
1961-62	.0213	.0555	.0514	.2107
1962-63	.0222	.0496	.0495	.1847
1963-64	.0208	.0542	.0505	.2073
1964-65	.0192	.0506	.0488	.1886
1965-66	.0192	.0473	.0473	.1761
1966-67	.0196	.0492	.0480	.1821
1967-68	.0192	.0515	.0496	.1886
1968-69	.0189	.0553	.0512	.2012
1969-70	.0196	.0513	.0503	.1863
1970-71	.0212	.0545	.0531	.1974
1971-72	.0204	.0612	.0576	.2106
1972-73	.0208	.0583	.0563	.2031
1973-74	.0196	.0579	.0552	.2017
1974-75	.0208	.0629	.0572	.2181
1975-76	.0204	.0536	.0505	.1966
1976-77	.0178	.0540	.0508	.2003
1977-78	.0188	.0525	.0496	.2002
1978-79	.0182	.0511	.0490	.1935
Mean	.0200	.0543	.0515	.1989
Standard deviation	.0012	.0041	.0030	.0120
Coefficient of variation	6.00%	7.55%	5.80%	6.03%

Source: Unpublished data.

tude of the CCI is in the lower range of the index scale. In essence, each measure leads to the same conclusions relating to the medium to low industry concentration and stability.

Each concentration index is independent of the total output of the industry. Hence, aggregate production increases (decreases) would not necessarily lead to changes in the market shares or the concentration indices. If the industry has shown major changes in the aggregate supplies, this added product must, however, be distributed among the processing capacity. The concentration patterns for Florida processors is especially interesting in light of the fact that substantial growth as well as instability has occurred in the industry's processed output. There has been no significant association between the dynamics of supply over time and the level of industry concentration. The largest firms' growth has been such that their shares of processed output have been relatively constant. The stability of the concentration measures has persisted, while the aggregate productive output of the industry has been unstable. It is again emphasized that the concentration indices are based on Florida supplies and do not include imported juice entering non-Florida ports.

Firm Entry and Exit

Citrus Processing Firms. The propensity for firm entry and exit provides important clues to structural barriers. Data on California and Texas were not available for totally assessing the extent of entry and exit. However, within the Sunkist organization the number of regional exchanges and local associations has remained fairly stable over the last decade. More detailed data are available with respect to Florida processors, and these data can be used to show the predominant conditions of entry and exit within the Florida processing phase of the industry. Both firm entry and exit have been evident in the processed citrus industry over the last two decades. Most if not all entry and exit has been among firms with smaller processing capacity.

An examination of the data on all firms over the periods from 1959–60 to 1978–79 reveals a diversity of firm entry and exit situations. Many firms entering the market operated for a few seasons and then became inoperative. Other firms entered the market and continued to grow. Finally, some firms already existing at the outset of the data period exited after a number of seasons of processing substantial volumes. These firms' activities can be analyzed by relating the incidence of entry and exit to firm market shares. Given the historical data on each firm over time, the propensity for firms of a given size to leave the industry or to grow can be evaluated using Markov processes, from which a transition matrix can be calculated. The transition matrix is based on data for Florida processors and does not include out-of-state processing and reprocessing operations.

The transition matrix shows the probability of a firm with a given market share moving from that share to another higher or lower market share (Table 2.6). Probabilities of movements from a given market share to share 0 indicate firm exit, while movements from share 0 to other shares show firm entry. Specifically, the first column is a measure of exit and the first row is a measure of entry (Table 2.6). The major diagonal values indicate the probability of firms remaining in the same category from one season to the next.

The results show that most Florida processors, especially the smaller firms, tend to remain in the same category. For example, there is an 81 percent probability that firms with 1 percent or less of the market output will maintain that market share. However, there is a 14 percent probability that the same firms will leave the industry. Finally, there is nearly a zero chance that the larger firms will exit as is evident from the zero values shown in column 0 (Table 2.6). In general, the larger firms show less of a propensity to maintain the same level over time. Yet most firms' market shares tend to fluctuate no more than 1 to 2 percent. This becomes evident from the cluster of values near the diagonal line.

Entry of new firms has been concentrated in the smaller size categories. When entry occurs, there is an 81 percent chance that the entering firm will have no more than 1 percent of the market.

Some further insights into the structure and trends in the structure can be gained from an examination of the rankings of the largest firms over time (Table 2.7). The two largest firms, while occasionally exchanging positions, always maintained a position in the three largest. The other member of the trio (Firm 49) started as the eighth largest in 1959–60 and became the largest in 1975–76. The remainder of the largest ten firms changed rankings more frequently, although they generally remained in the top ten Florida processors.

Reconstitution Operations. All bulk orange concentrate must be reconstituted into retail and institutional pack juices. Most of the medium to large Florida processors produce, store, and reconstitute bulk orange juice. An increasing share of Florida bulk concentrate is shipped out of state in bulk form. Likewise, nearly all imported juice is in bulk form. Several new entries into the reprocessing industry have taken place. Ex-

Table 2.6. Markov transition matrix for Florida citrus processors.

	Index of projected market share[a]

	0	1	2	3	4	5	6	7	8	9	10	11	12	13	14
					Probability of a firm changing market share										
0	.9333	.0540	.0037	.0030	.0015	.0007	.0022	.0015	0	0	0	0	0	0	0
1	.1378	.8079	.0459	.0021	.0021	.0042	0	0	0	0	0	0	0	0	0
2	.0420	.1469	.6294	.1608	.0140	0	0	.0070	0	0	0	0	0	0	0
3	.0236	.0315	.1890	.6299	.0945	.0157	.0157	0	0	0	0	0	0	0	0
4	.0	.0250	.0250	.2750	.4250	.2500	0	0	0	0	0	0	0	0	0
5	.0492	.0328	0	.0492	.1148	.6557	.0820	0	0	.0164	0	0	0	0	0
6	.0370	0	0	.0741	0	.2593	.4444	.1852	0	0	0	0	0	0	0
7	.0588	.0588	0	0	0	0	.2353	.4706	.1765	0	0	0	0	0	0
8	.2000	0	0	0	0	0	0	.2000	.4000	0	0	.2000	0	0	0
9	.0	0	0	0	.1667	0	.1667	0	0	.1667	0	0	0	0	0
10	.0	0	0	0	0	0	0	0	0	0	.5000	0	0	0	0
11	.0	0	0	0	0	0	0	0	.1111	.2222	.2222	.2222	.2222	0	0
12	.0	0	0	0	0	0	0	0	0	0	.2222	.2222	.3333	.2222	0
13	.0	0	0	0	0	0	0	0	0	0	.2308	.1538	.3846	.1538	.0769
14	.0	0	0	0	0	0	0	0	0	.2000	0	0	.4000	.2000	.2000

Source: Unpublished data.
Note: Base years for transition probabilities are 1959-60 and 1978-79.

[a]

0 = 0	5 = .04 < $\bar{X}$ < .05	10 = .09 < $\bar{X}$ < .10
1 = 0 < $\bar{X}$ < .01	6 = .05 < $\bar{X}$ < .06	11 = .10 < $\bar{X}$ < .11
2 = .01 < $\bar{X}$ < .02	7 = .06 < $\bar{X}$ < .07	12 = .11 < $\bar{X}$ < .12
3 = .02 < $\bar{X}$ < .03	8 = .07 < $\bar{X}$ < .08	13 = .12 < $\bar{X}$ < .13
4 = .03 < $\bar{X}$ < .04	9 = .08 < $\bar{X}$ < .09	14 = .13 < $\bar{X}$ < .14

Table 2.7   Rankings of the largest citrus processing firms during the seasons 1959-60 through 1978-79.

FIRM RANK
(1 = largest)

Season	1 Firm code	1 Market share	2 Firm code	2 Market share	3 Firm code	3 Market share	4 Firm code	4 Market share	5 Firm code	5 Market share	6 Firm code	6 Market share	7 Firm code	7 Market share	8 Firm code	8 Market share	9 Firm code	9 Market share	10 Firm code	10 Market share
78-79	49	.1242	34	.0905	8	.0769	7	.0588	23	.0492	26	.0448	50	.0443	14	.0436	1	.0364	109	.0328
77-78	49	.1321	34	.0910	8	.0768	7	.0543	50	.0470	23	.0453	26	.0430	14	.0373	109	.0367	22	.0355
76-77	49	.1269	8	.0986	34	.0839	7	.0556	50	.0528	23	.0441	1	.0433	39	.0421	22	.0405	26	.0357
75-76	49	.1213	34	.0987	8	.0894	7	.0604	50	.0584	39	.0427	1	.0425	23	.0384	22	.0383	14	.0320
74-75	8	.1296	34	.1139	49	.1031	23	.0806	50	.0604	9	.0446	39	.0413	1	.0400	15	.0350	31	.0309
73-74	8	.1160	34	.0987	49	.0980	23	.0808	50	.0647	39	.0461	15	.0454	9	.0441	1	.0438	106	.0310
72-73	8	.1172	34	.1128	49	.0949	50	.0649	7	.0615	1	.0459	14	.0450	23	.0407	39	.0398	22	.0366
71-72	8	.1210	34	.1154	49	.1000	50	.0728	7	.0644	39	.0469	1	.0453	14	.0406	23	.0401	22	.0355
70-71	8	.1195	34	.1016	49	.0774	50	.0631	7	.0627	39	.0491	1	.0486	23	.0469	22	.0386	14	.0377
69-70	8	.1105	34	.1000	49	.0766	50	.0630	7	.0598	39	.0482	23	.0428	1	.0412	14	.0381	22	.0345
68-69	34	.1243	8	.1153	49	.0672	7	.0604	50	.0522	39	.0495	1	.0482	23	.0446	22	.0436	14	.0286
67-68	8	.1142	34	.1032	49	.0617	7	.0695	50	.0559	39	.0531	22	.0455	23	.0413	1	.0406	14	.0311
66-67	34	.1101	8	.1012	7	.0660	50	.0578	49	.0537	39	.0521	23	.0442	10	.0428	1	.0404	43	.0294
65-66	8	.1059	34	.0941	7	.0591	50	.0588	49	.0575	39	.0493	10	.0447	23	.0438	67	.0397	1	.0390
64-65	8	.1171	34	.1039	50	.0631	10	.0553	39	.0540	7	.0496	23	.0438	49	.0432	1	.0413	43	.0326
63-64	8	.1401	34	.0968	50	.0604	39	.0540	23	.0514	7	.0504	82	.0467	49	.0414	1	.0364	31	.0333
62-63	8	.1132	34	.0894	89	.0706	23	.0551	49	.0547	7	.0542	50	.0484	39	.0478	1	.0407	43	.0394
61-62	8	.1424	34	.0975	89	.0664	50	.0570	7	.0509	39	.0483	1	.0455	49	.0403	43	.0342	20	.0289
60-61	8	.1488	34	.1126	89	.0592	50	.0529	7	.0487	39	.0471	1	.0444	20	.0440	49	.0372	43	.0359
59-60	8	.1377	34	.1067	89	.0811	50	.0529	7	.0466	1	.0451	39	.0438	49	.0394	20	.0365	43	.0355

Source: Unpublished data.

isting dairy plant facilities can be readily adapted to the reprocessing of orange juice. These firms are directly involved in pricing, promotion, and competing for shelf space. Large retail chains can easily contract with these processors for their private labels. This growth in out-of-state processing has directly reduced the market power and price leadership that was historically exerted by Florida processors. The power implied with the Lorenz curve (Figure 2.3) has clearly declined even though the measured Lorenz curves have remained fairly stable. Data on out-of-state processing are not available to allow similar concentration indices to be calculated for the total United States.

Packinghouses. Statistics similar to those for Florida processors are published for Florida fresh packers. Transition matrices were calculated for fresh Florida grapefruit. Similar data were not available to the authors for calculating transition matrices for Texas and California. A discussion of the Florida fresh sector is included to provide some empirical evidence of structural adjustments in the fresh sector, although the omission of the other significant producing regions is recognized.

A comparison of firms' entry and exit for the Indian River and interior districts is shown in Table 2.8. Given that firms do enter the market, then the probability that these new firms will be of the smallest size categories is greater in the interior district, that is, firms entering the interior district tend to be smaller than new Indian River firms. The probabilities in both columns 2 and 3 of Table 2.8 establish in both cases

Table 2.8   The probabilities that Florida fresh citrus packers enter and exit the industry from various size categories for each district.

Size Category Thousands of 4/5 bushel boxes	Probability that packer enters the market with a given initial shipment volume		Probability that a packinghouse of a given size will exit from the market	
	Indian River	Interior	Indian River	Interior
1–150	.5859	.8304	.8379	.7770
150–300	.0980	.0368	.1935	.1707
300–600	.1707	.0804	.1804	.2471
600–960	.0606	.0223	.0961	.0000
960–1,288	.0727	.0223	.1213	.0218
over 1,288	.0121	.0078	.0000	.1110

Source: Calculated from Division of Fruit and Vegetable Inspection.

the low occurrence of new firms shipping sizeable volumes the first season. However, the Indian River district does show 41 percent of entering firms shipping 150,000 or more ⅘ bushel boxes the first year.

Firms exiting from the industry can be further compared. Given that a firm does change from its initial size, then the probability that such a firm completely exits from the market can be determined. These values are shown in columns 4 and 5 of Table 2.8. Over 83 percent of the smallest Indian River firms which make adjustments between the categories actually exit the industry. The probability of exit is slightly lower for small firms in the interior. In contrast, the probability of complete firm exit among the larger interior firms who make size adjustments exceeds the comparable values calculated for the Indian River district.

In general, among those firms making structural adjustments in their shipment levels, interior firms both enter and exit primarily within the smaller size categories (less than 600,000 boxes) with one exception noted in the exit of larger firms. In contrast, the entry of Indian River firms is spread over all size categories and exits over the smaller five or six categories.

Industry Progressiveness. At the grove level, producers have experimented with mechanical harvesters. The harvester adoption has been slow because of the lower cost of labor relative to mechanization. With governmental emphasis on improving the economically disadvantaged migrant worker and with the possibility of unionization, labor will become more expensive in the future. The adoption of mechanical harvesters will be closely correlated with the future price of labor.

Adoption of mechanization in packinghouses has also been slow primarily because of relatively inexpensive labor. Workers are paid on a piece rate basis and receive no pay when fruit is not available for packing. Labor is a more flexible resource than capital in an industry that has varying daily volumes to pack and a season that averages 35 weeks per year. The old technologies that utilize labor are not complex and can be used with proper maintenance. Thus, the decision to mechanize is complicated by projected cost of labor in the future.

The deviation of individual firms from average sector cost is an indication of improvement in industry cost efficiency. Since 1971 the sector has improved its technical efficiency, as evidenced by the decrease in the coefficient of variation of cost among firms (Table 2.9). The trend will likely continue in this sector as competition among packinghouses causes firms to minimize costs.

Table 2.9. The coefficient of variation of packinghouse and pick and haul cost among Florida firms, 1970-71 through 1982-83.

Year	Packinghouse[a]	Picking and hauling[b]
1970-71	17.7%	13.9%
1971-72	14.5	11.5
1972-73	17.5	09.9
1973-74	15.1	10.6
1974-75	13.6	10.5
1975-76	13.2	10.7
1976-77	16.8	9.8
1977-78	17.6	15.3
1978-79	13.6	16.0
1979-80	15.7	15.0
1980-81	12.2	13.8
1981-82	14.8	16.9
1982-83	-	20.7

Source: [a]Hooks, various issues (a); Hooks and Kilmer, various issues (a).
[b]Hooks and Spurlock, various issues; Hooks, various issues (b).

Processing plants are highly mechanized operations. Evaporators are the key constraining feature that determines plant capacity. With large fixed costs, reduction of variable cost becomes very important. In 1982–83 cans represented 40 percent of total processing and selling cost. A number of processors have individually or jointly invested in can-producing plants in order to reduce costs.

Processing adds time utility to citrus, which allows consumption to occur throughout the year. Once the product is in a storable form, storage, handling, and transportation become important areas for cost reduction. Instead of storing the transformed product in 55-gallon drums, new bulk storage is being adopted. Also, bulk distribution of concentrate out of state has increased from 18 percent of frozen concentrated orange juice in 1975–76 to 49 percent in 1985–86 (Florida Canners Association, *Statistical Summary*).

Along with attempts to reduce marketing costs, the industry has adopted an aggressive marketing program designed both to stimulate consumers and to measure their preferences. These programs have resulted in a variety of products and sizes and types of containers intended to meet the broad array of orange juice consumer demands.

The examples above identify but a few activities suggesting that the citrus industry is highly progressive, especially in terms of marketing innovations and organizational arrangements. Programs to disseminate information, to coordinate inventories, to advertise products, and to organize central selling, particularly, point to the level of innovativeness at the free on board (f.o.b.) processor/packer level. Industry-imposed regulations with minimal governmental input suggest that the industry is highly progressive in its abilities to independently adopt those controls necessary for the welfare of the industry. Likewise, both the development of research programs and the utilization of research findings throughout the industry point to a high level of progressiveness.

Competitive Environment in the Industry. The processor has been the most powerful participant in the vertical market channel. With a decline in number of buyers facing the processor (narrowing markets) and the corresponding increase in quantity demanded by each retailer, the balance of power is shifting away from the processor. As markets narrow, they then become closed to other processors, which further decreases the number of buyers and sellers in a particular market. The narrowing of markets is further enhanced as the popularity of private labels increases. As a larger percentage of processor output goes to a retailer, the bargaining power of the retailer is improved relative to that of the processor. Retailers can enlist other processors whereas processors may find it difficult to enlist other retailers. The balance of power in the vertical market channel of the citrus industry is changing and will continue to change in the future. This area of change in the vertical structure needs further theoretical and empirical analysis for the entire industry.

3

•
•
•
•
•
•
•
•
•
•
•

Citrus Market Channels

Production and Market Channels

Production and Marketing Stages in Florida. Citrus production generally represents substantial capital investments in lands, trees, inputs, and ultimately harvesting. After the initial investment in a new grove, at least five years are usually required before the trees begin bearing marketable fruit with yields large enough to cover the cost of production and harvesting. However, recent higher density planting may yield earlier returns where more trees per acre are harvested with a lower yield per tree. Given this relatively long time span before significant returns from the production can be expected, the rate of entry and exit by producers is usually low and adjustments in acreage are relatively stable over time. The Florida freezes have altered these traditions somewhat; however, in their absence the tradition holds.

Once the groves are bearing, the first stage beyond that of production management is coordination of harvesting. Citrus harvesting differs slightly by regions; California's season usually extends farther into the summer months. In all supply areas harvesting time varies by variety. Harvesting is accomplished in one of three ways. First, the grove owner may totally coordinate picking crews and other harvesting functions. Second, private companies providing caretaking and harvesting services may be utilized. Finally, caretaking services may be provided to members of a cooperative or some other arrangement whereby fruit is sold under a nonpricing or pooling agreement.

Most citrus is delivered to either packinghouses or processors, depending on the intent of utilization. Packinghouses provide the assembling, washing, grading, and packaging for the fresh market, and eliminations are diverted to processing. Citrus used for processing is cleaned and processed into canned, chilled, or concentrate, while by-products are diverted into cattle feeds, cosmetics, food additives, and so forth.

Generally, the selling functions are provided by the packers and processors. Primary differences in the organizational structure of the major producing regions occur at this stage. Florida producers send their fruit destined for fresh markets to both private and cooperative packinghouses. These houses provide the normal packing services and may provide the selling functions. Packers that have their own selling forces maintain control over the free on board (f.o.b.) distribution of their fresh fruit. Alternatively, a Florida packer may be a member of a control selling exchange (one example is Sealdsweet) which provides the selling and coordinating functions for its members. Buy bids are received by the exchange and are then coordinated with different packers. Fruit is sold under the exchange label and/or the packinghouse label. Buy orders may be restricted to certain packinghouse labels designated by the buyer. Hence, while a central exchange is used for selling, it is still possible for members to maintain some degree of product identity.

Production and Marketing Stages in California. In contrast to the Florida system where numerous private labels exist among packers, most California producers are members of Sunkist Growers Cooperative. Sunkist includes member growers, local associations, district exchanges, and affiliated fruit grower supply companies. A local association is a nonprofit cooperative association of growers. It represents its members in the district exchange and in Sunkist Growers, Inc., and usually provides packing services. Local associations provide facilities for assembling, washing, grading, and preparing growers' fruit for market. Here fruit is physically pooled, and final pooling and distribution of proceeds is made to growers. The growers who use licensed packers are restricted to picking, packing, and shipping fruit as authorized by Sunkist Growers, Inc. All marketing functions for these growers are conferred on the district exchange and Sunkist Growers, Inc.

A packinghouse is the direct point of contact with the grower for most activities associated with citrus production. In addition to regular functions, some packing units perform certain orchard services for growers, including pruning, frost protection, fumigating, and spraying.

Most associations require growers to rely on the packing unit for harvesting so that fruit can be picked by expert crews.

In most cases packing units make arrangements for transportation of fruit from the orchard. At the packinghouse citrus goes through numerous operations, including washing, drying, grading, and sizing. Experienced graders visually separate fruit into classes according to specific requirements for various grades. Fruit is either weighed or automatically counted after leaving the grading area. A record is made of the quantities of various sizes and grades each grower sends to the packinghouse. Citrus thus becomes part of a pooling system under which individual growers receive payment according to grades and sizes furnished.

Each packing unit or affiliated packinghouse uses its own trademarks called house brands. This enables the produce trade to identify fruit from particular packinghouses as well as from different geographical areas. Each house brand is assigned to a particular grade of fruit established by Sunkist. If a packinghouse brand is used in connection with, for example, a lower grade fruit, the packing unit is precluded from using that same house brand for premium quality fruit. A packing unit may use one or more house brands in connection with premium fruit, one or more house brands for lower grade fruit, and so on.

Each of the district exchanges in the Sunkist organization is a nonprofit cooperative association comprised of growers who have their fruit packed by licensed packers, or of associations of growers operating as local associations, or both. The exchanges have direct involvement for grower members in representation and voting, in handling and distributing sales proceeds, and in allocating property rights. District exchanges reserve the right of final decision on price (except auction sales), destination, and transportation after the sale has been made by Sunkist. Growers and local associations delegate these rights to the exchanges in accordance with the bylaws of Sunkist Growers, Inc. Finally, for all producing regions, nearly all fresh fruit has been sold under an f.o.b. packinghouse transaction. The buyer's contact is with the independent packer, the centralized exchange, or the district sales offices within the Sunkist system.

Citrus Processing Stages.   In the processing sector considerable differences are apparent among the major supply regions. Within the California system most processed sales are coordinated through the Sunkist organizational structure, which is similar to that used for fresh marketing. In contrast, Florida's overall marketing structure includes a variety of independent and related structural arrangements. Some packers are affiliated with processors, while others are totally independent.

With only a few exceptions, marketing of Florida processed citrus is completed by the individual processors. Most processors maintain a large sales staff and provide various supply contracting arrangements with producers. Most processed products are sold under either brands or private label. A large share of brand sales are made through nonpriced contractual arrangements with the major food retail chains. Each Florida processor makes the decision as to the extent of product differentiation within its operation, the nature of its selling activities, the types of products produced, and storage decisions. However, the market structure of the industry prevents these decisions from being made independently of other processors.

Processors are the major decision-making forces within the Florida citrus industry. They provide most of the producer pooling arrangements and are directly responsible for pricing and selling processed citrus. Marketing policies ultimately determine the level of f.o.b. returns, which in turn determine the returns to the different producer pooling arrangements. Some processors are sole members of a central selling exchange that provides selling and coordinating functions for some processed citrus products. Finally, processed citrus is distributed to either primary or secondary markets. Primary markets include the retail outlets and are usually supplied through direct sales to large chains, sales to large independents, and sales coordinated through brokers. Secondary markets include schools, institutional outlets, and export markets. These sales are often contracted directly with processors and selling organizations specializing in secondary market trade.

Overall, three broad stages of production and marketing have been briefly identified. Once production decisions are made, producers must arrange for harvesting and pricing their product. Fruit moves from the groves to either packing or processing facilities; product transformation, pricing, selling, and storage functions are performed at this stage. Finally, the product distribution function is completed with linkages between the packer or processor and the retail and institutional outlets. Generally this represents transformation in time and space only, since most citrus products are produced in their final consumable form at the packer or processor level. One significant exception to this would be the f.o.b. distribution of bulk frozen concentrate, part of which is distributed to reconstitution facilities outside the regulatory control of the various producing regions.

Volume through Channels

Movements of oranges and grapefruit are illustrated in Figures 3.1.a and 3.1.b where each producing region's contribution to the industry is given. The predominance of Florida in both orange and grapefruit production is clearly evident. Similarly, the significance of California in supplying fresh oranges is shown where 75 percent of the industry's fresh orange supplies are from California.

A more detailed analysis of the vertical market system for Florida oranges and grapefruit is shown in Figures 3.2.a and 3.2.b. Of the estimated 8,169 Florida growers producing oranges nearly 67 percent of their supplies are marketed under either a cooperative arrangement or through participation pooling plans provided by private processors (Florida Canners Association). Hence, the bulk of Florida oranges are sold under an arrangement in which the marketing functions and decisions are established by processors. Returns to the pools, whether private or cooperative, represent the residual after the cost and profits of the processing operations have been determined. In the case of cooperatives the grower maintains some input in establishing processor marketing policies, but when selling through private participation plans or spot markets, the grower relinquishes all decision-making authority.

Over 98 percent of the fresh citrus is sold by packinghouses directly to retail and institutional outlets (Figures 3.2.a and 3.2.b). The outlets have grown over time, while the terminal auction percentage volume has declined. Processing functions are more relevant to Florida, since 96 percent of the oranges and 61 percent of all grapefruit are processed. Processing functions are nearly identical for all plants, since the products are highly standardized through quality controls and regulations. However, selling functions differ depending on the extent of private labels (i.e., retail chain labels) versus brands. Approximately 35 to 50 percent of all orange juices are sold under brands while the remaining juices are packed as private labels. For frozen concentrate, the percentage is 22 percent for brands and 78 percent for private labels (NPD Research, Inc.). Recent trends have been toward an increase in brand share for all orange juices.

Frozen concentrate accounts for the largest amount of processed orange juice and grapefruit juice (Figures 3.2.a and 3.2.b). Approximately 80 percent of the frozen orange concentrate flows directly to the retail markets, 10 percent goes to the institutional markets, and an estimated 10 percent is shipped in bulk form. Recent growth in the bulk market indicates an increase in the amount of concentrate being shipped from Florida and then reprocessed out of state along with the reprocess-

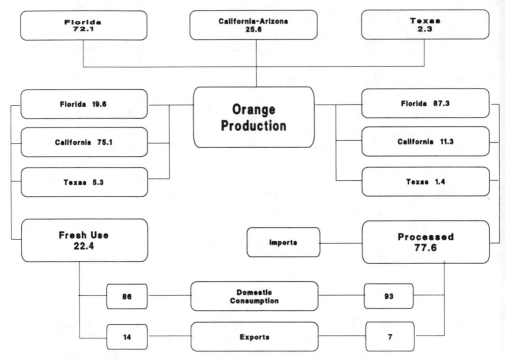

Figure 3.1.a. Vertical structure and regional shares by percentage of oranges,
1978–79 through 1983–84.

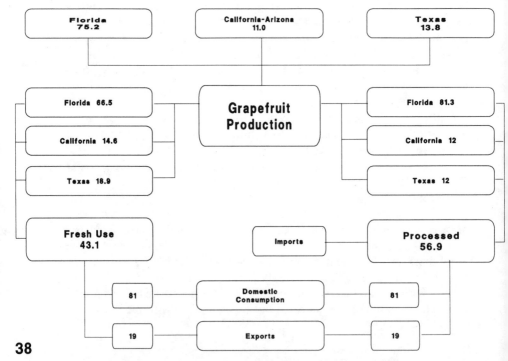

Figure 3.1.b. Vertical structure and regional shares by percentage of grapefruit,
1978–79 through 1983–84.

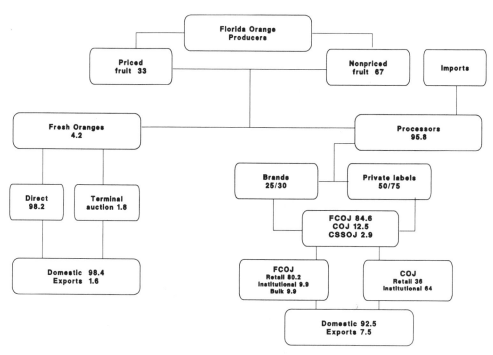

Figure 3.2.a. Stages of production and distribution of Florida oranges by percentage, average for 1979–80 through 1983–84.

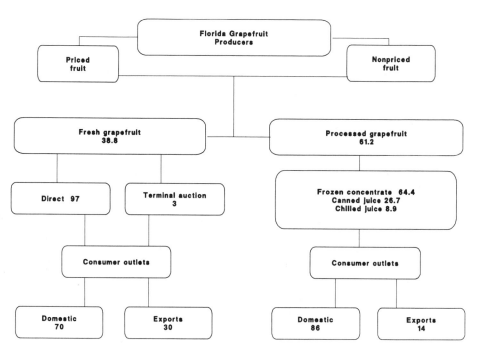

Figure 3.2.b. Distribution of Florida grapefruit by percentage through the vertical market structure, 1979–80 through 1983–84.

ing of imported juices. In-state shipments of bulk have increased (Florida Canners Association, *Statistical Summary*). This indicates a change has occurred in who performs certain transformation functions within the vertical system. This change has created considerable concern among processors over loss of quality control. Nearly 64 percent of the chilled juices is in institutional pack, with the remainder sold in retail containers (Florida Canners Association, *Statistical Summary*). Statistics on canned juices show a predominance of retail packs of different container sizes.

Coordinating the Market Flow

While a number of different structural arrangements exist to form the vertical market structure of the citrus industry, the overall complexity of coordination is not greatly different among the three major domestic producing regions. In contrast to many U.S. agricultural commodities citrus is produced in what can be considered as highly localized production regions. The regionalization of production and the clearly delineated control and regulation within each region does simplify the coordinating task. This is especially true for the linkage between producers and first handlers. The dominant cooperative system of California and the nonprice exchange mechanisms (e.g., contracts, cooperatives, and vertical integration) in Florida have evolved as the major modes for coordination between producers and first handlers.

With the increased importance of large retail chains, the coordination complexity between packers and/or processors with retail outlets may have decreased. Processors dealing directly with large retail outlets rather than through many small brokers may have a better estimate of expected purchases and can more readily package products to meet retail outlet demands.

Product allocation and storage decisions generally create the most difficult coordination features. Both supply and demand for citrus is seasonal. In order to meet seasonal demands, especially at the beginning of a new crop year, it is necessary to project current supplies and movements and then maintain sufficient inventories of concentrate for the beginning of the next year. If a portion of the crop is lost due to poor weather the inventories may become too low. Similarly, if production exceeds current projections, inventories may become excessive. In either circumstance the coordination of inventories can be the major factor leading to a financially successful season for the processing phase of the industry.

The industry has little control over major losses due to severe freezes, which cause supply variability. However, the current market structure does often facilitate salvaging freeze-damaged fruit which can be used for processed citrus. Usually the cooperatives and private processors have contingency plans for immediately harvesting damaged fruit after severe freezes. Processing technology has greatly reduced the total losses that would normally be expected from such severe weather. Of course, product quantity originally destined for fresh markets is reduced in these situations.

The citrus industry is a major leader among agricultural industries in conducting programs to stimulate demand. While regional competition, growth in income, and some product substitution influence demand, the industry can fairly accurately project the demand for both fresh and processed products. These projections, in turn, are used to coordinate the inventory levels over time.

Data on the market structure among processors indicated that the industry is oligopolistic. Hence, the actions of one processor may lead to reactions by others. If one processor's inventories become excessive relative to other competitors, that processor may try to implement corrective measures through price-cutting and/or various buyer incentive programs. Usually these actions will lead to immediate responses by the other processors. In recent crop years, inventories have not been a problem. While this is only one of many examples of coordination problems, it does illustrate how decisions by one large processor may immediately influence the entire industry. If a large processor is committed to too many participation contracts relative to projected sales, then the situation described above can easily occur. In general these types of coordinating problems will occur at the processor rather than packer level, simply because excess fresh fruit can be diverted to processing.

Coordination at the First Handler Level. Throughout the prior discussion, the coordination between producers and first handlers has been shown to be accomplished with both priced and nonpriced arrangements. In this section we will look at these arrangements in more detail with specific emphasis given to participation plans, cooperatives, and spot prices.

PARTICIPATION PLANS. Marketing through a participation plan includes many of the features of cooperative marketing. It is usually the private corporation that offers a participation plan, but such a plan may also be offered by a cooperative. Participation plans are contractual arrangements between growers and handlers. It is also a deferred pricing alternative, since the final price is not determined until after the product has been sold and the fruit or product pool closed.

Participation plans differ from cooperatives in that there are no retained earnings returned to the growers. The packing or processing facilities are not owned by the grower; hence there is not a deduction for capital expenditure funds. The price realized for the product depends upon the returns from marketing the product and the method of price determination or terms of the contract. The marketing decisions are made by corporation management, and seldom does the grower have any influence upon the pricing policies of the packer or processor. In addition, the grower remains in the position of being the residual claimant who bears the risk of price changes; the packer or processor will receive payment for carrying out its functions, with the grower receiving the excess pool revenues after expenses. This favors the grower when prices are high, but works against the grower in other years.

When marketing fruit through a participation plan, the grower is assured a home for the fruit, which is especially beneficial should there be a freeze or extreme product surplus. The grower does not have to be concerned with timing deliveries to get the highest price for products. Should prices advance because of a freeze, the grower will still share in higher postfreeze prices because the average or pool price will advance.

In a participation plan, final payment for fruit may occur a considerable time after the fruit is delivered. The grower may have months or even up to a year and a half to wait until the product is sold and the pool is closed. However, there are usually incremental payments or advances made to the fruit in the pooled arrangement.

In general, there are two types of participation plan contracts. Under production contracts, the buyer takes all of the production from a grove. Under a limit contract the quantity to be delivered is specified. Examples of production contracts with and without price provisions are illustrated in Tables 3.1 and 3.2. Limit contracts would be similar except they include details on quantities to be delivered. A third type of contract includes a minimum guaranteed price in return for longer term commitments.

SPOT MARKET. To price fruit at the time of harvest or delivery is to sell in the spot market. This means not committing fruit to any buyer until harvesttime. During seasons when the inventories of processed products are adequate and the crop size is nominal to heavy, the cash seller will usually have to sell fruit at a substantial discount to other methods of marketing fruit. However, if inventories are low, if crop size is small or

Table 3.1. Examples of alternative participation plans with price provisions specified.

Price provisions	Firm A participation agreement	Firm B participation agreement	Firm C participation agreement
Variety-product pools	1. Early and mids 2. Valencias	1. Early and mids 2. Valencias	Fresh and by variety, cannery pool
Pool period	1. Dec.15-Apr.15 2. Apr.15-Oct.15	1. Early and mids 2. Valencias	Monthly pools except for 2-week pools at beginning of season
Revenues	Average selling price of firm (f.o.b. Lakeland)	Weighted average of industry nonad[a] f.o.b. price adjusted for FCA FCOJ cash price average, premium of not less than 3%	Sales
Costs	Packing, processing, selling, administrative-22.5%	Packaging, other cost	Actual packing and marketing costs. Handling and eliminating costs. Other costs applicable to fruit 15/box service charge
Payment basis	Pound solids	Pound solids	Fresh: Boxes
By-products	--	In lieu of processing fees, retains, or service fees. Firm B accepts	--
Price guarantees	--	--	--
Limit or production contract	Production	Production	Production
Quantity credit	--	--	Account for: fresh fruit, packed boxes received, total boxes delivered direct to plant

Source: Niles (1979).
[a]Nonadvertised.

reduced because of a freeze, or if demand increases during the season, the late season spot seller's return will be at a premium to the return from other marketing options.

Spot sales can be made to any buyer needing citrus fruit. These buyers can be processors, fresh packers, gift fruit operators, roadside

Table 3.2. Examples of alternative participation plans with nonprice provisions specified.

Nonprice provisions	Firm A participation agreement	Firm B participation agreement	Firm C participation agreement
Advances			
a) pick haul/ initial payment	Within 2 weeks of delivery, not to exceed 65% of projected revenues	80% of lesser weekly FCA cash price of FCA seasonal to date	Agreed upon pick & haul (no interest)
b) additional payment	--	--	Fresh: 80% of estimated returns on or before 60 days after close of each pool. Cannery: June 15, 30% Sept. 15, 30% Dec. 15, 30% Mar. 15, balance
c) final payment	Within 15 days of pool closing	Within 15 days of pool closing	Fresh: as soon as possible after audit of fiscal year closing August 31
d) time of contracting	--	--	--
e) further advances	--	--	--
Services	Harvesting	--	Picking and hauling
Fruit quality standards	Minimum state federal	Brix acid ratio not less than 12:1, Min. 10 Brix individual load basis. No late bloom	State and federal inspection and individual load basis
Picking of delivery schedule	--	Firm B specifies	--
Termination	Notification during June	--	--
Failure to deliver	25¢/box	25¢/box	50¢/box

Source: Niles (1979).

markets, or bird dogs. The price received in the spot market will largely be set by the buyer and will be determined mainly by the quality of fruit offered for sale. The buyer's price is usually related both to the immediate supply and demand for fruit in the local area and to the buyer's particular situation.

The payment for fruit priced at delivery is immediate. However, since a home for the fruit has not been assured it may be difficult to get the fruit harvested and delivered at desirable times such as during the period immediately following a freeze. Here the price would be heavily discounted because others are attempting to deliver as much fruit as possible, and buyers are offering lower prices. Should the fruit be sold at this time or prior to a freeze, the seller would not benefit from the higher freeze prices.

COOPERATIVES. Cooperative marketing is the extension of the grower's business activity into the packing, processing, and selling of the product. When a grower places fruit in a cooperative, the grower is assured of an outlet for the fruit. This can be important after a freeze, when it is imperative to get the fruit harvested and delivered as soon as possible. Having an assured home is also desirable during surplus crop seasons. The grower is no longer concerned about the timing of deliveries in order to receive the highest price, because the fruit is pooled with that of other growers, and an average price is paid. These returns should reflect both revenues generated from sales of the primary product as well as by-products.

The grower can also benefit from the services provided through grove caretaking, picking and hauling, and in some cases, even financial assistance. In most cases the grower maintains no control over the price received for the fruit, but entrusts the management of the cooperative with marketing the fruit. The price that the grower receives for fruit is based upon the selling price of the final product minus the expenses of the cooperative. The grower shares in the net returns in proportion to the grower's contribution.

There are four types of cooperative associations in the citrus industry. The first type, the fresh fruit packinghouse cooperative, channels fruit into the fresh market. Packinghouse eliminations and direct shipment from the growers usually go to a second type of cooperative, the cooperative processor. Packinghouse cooperatives are usually members of a cooperative processor, but grower members can also deliver their fruit to the processor. The third type of organization, the centralized cooperative, receives both fresh and processed fruit. Centralized cooperatives that do only selling also exist in both the fresh and processed segments of the industry. The last type is the cooperative fruit association that is affiliated with an independent corporation which processes and markets the products from the fruit.

The grower's share of the revenues from the sale of product depends upon pooling arrangements of the cooperative. Pooling can be described as a method of combining the deliveries of the member's fruit into groups with similar characteristics. Pooling is carried out to avoid having to keep each grower's fruit separate as it is packed, processed, and marketed. In most cases an individual grower's identity is lost once the fruit has been delivered and unloaded. However, the quantity and quality characteristics are determined from samples taken by state inspectors or from actually determining the grade and size.

All fruit of the same variety, or for use in the same end product, is placed in the same pool. During the season or selected pool period the appropriate revenues and costs charged to a pool are accumulated. At the end of the season or pool period the pools are closed and the grower is paid on the basis of his or her contribution to the pool.

Cooperatives, being owned by the growers, distribute all of the earnings from marketing the members' fruit. Each pool is allocated revenue from sales of the product. All expenses or assessments are charged to the individual pools by methods established by the cooperative. In the case of cooperative fruit associations, for example, contractual arrangements between the cooperative and the affiliated corporation specify the items to be credited and deducted. By-product credit may be specified for processing and for administering the association. Certain price guarantees may also be included.

MARKETING ORDERS. Marketing orders play an important role in the U.S. citrus economy in several ways, depending on the type of orders under consideration. Two types of orders are in place. First there are several federal marketing orders in California-Arizona, Florida, and Texas. They are defined for grapefruit and oranges, with the orange orders defined for specific varieties. In addition, Florida has a state marketing order that provides unique coordination functions to that section of the citrus industry. To understand the importance of marketing orders as a coordinating mechanism, it is essential that these two types of orders be discussed separately.

Federal orders for citrus provide three primary coordinating functions: grades and standards, volume management and market flow, and market support activities. The federal orders are limited to dealing with fresh marketing activities, hence their importance clearly differs by region. In Chapter 1 it was noted that California is predominantly a fresh oriented market while Florida's citrus is mostly used for processing. Thus regulatory control over California citrus through the marketing orders would be expected to be a more important coordinating tool than for Florida. In fact, there has been considerable controversy over the extensive use of the California order in the last several seasons (Mueller et al. 1987).

Citrus federal orders provide regional control of the quality, size, and packaging of fresh citrus entering the interstate marketing channels. Such regulations have contributed to maintaining high quality throughout the crop year as well as providing a mechanism for achieving some regional product differentiation. For example, Indian River grapefruit is a well-recognized regional brand that is associated with the Indian River marketing order region. This order has helped the region maintain quality controls and packaging and labeling standards.

The citrus federal orders do not provide direct control over volume. Rather the orders can be used to manage volume during certain periods of the harvest season via prorates and shipping holidays. Prorates is a mechanism where the maximum volume of fruit to leave the order within a week can be defined. During the pro rata periods extending over several weeks of the harvest season, a maximum volume of fruit to be shipped is defined. Then each packinghouse is allowed a pro rata share of the total volume. The primary purpose of this supply management activity is to prevent excessive supplies from building up at the wholesale and retail markets. Fresh citrus is perishable and excessive supplies could lead to quality deterioration that may damage longer term consumption behavior, especially if the consumer purchases spoiled fruit.

Shipping holidays have much the same function as prorates except that they prohibit shipments completely following certain holidays. Large shipments of fresh fruit generally precede major fall holidays such as Thanksgiving and Christmas. Sales usually drop off dramatically after these dates. The shipment holidays are simply designed to prevent excessive buildup of perishable fruits following these holidays. Both types of volume controls are intended not to regulate supplies but to prevent poorer quality fruit from reaching the consumer.

Recent controversy over the volume management activities in California stem from the potential use of the order beyond the coordinating flow to market function. Cases can be cited where the secretary of agriculture has suspended the order because of potential abuse.

In addition to Florida's federal citrus orders the Florida citrus industry has a state order that greatly expands the regulatory control over the Florida industry. Specifically, the Florida state order applies to all fruit produced and/or shipped from Florida in either fresh or processed form. The order provides for direct taxing authority on citrus production to generate funds to support the market coordinating functions. The Florida state order is probably the most significant institutional structure found within the U.S. citrus economy because it provides the legal framework for the Florida Citrus Commission. Through the commission, the Florida industry not only regulates quality and standards but also implements a national and international generic promotional program for the industry. Most of the funds collected are used to support the generic promotion activities and associated market coordinating functions, including scientific, marketing, and economic research.

Marketing orders are an integral part of the U.S. citrus economy in coordinating the quality standards and providing consumers with information about the range of products via advertising. The orders do not allow the industry to collectively become involved in the exchange process. That is, the marketing orders do not provide any authority for buying and selling as they are currently defined. Using the state order to develop a reserve pool of processed fruit, which has been discussed but not implemented, would be one exception to the exchange function. The reserve pool concept when considered was designed to provide the industry greater control over the storage functions. However, changes in supply conditions over the years were such that the concept was never fully debated.

While the marketing orders cover several functions, in general the control over qualities and the ability to support national generic advertising programs are the most significant. Other agricultural industries such as dairy and honey have turned to national legislation that gives them the authority to mount national advertising programs. Up to this point Florida has accounted for enough of the industry that it could justify supporting the national and international efforts. Recent expansions in imports into the U.S. market will likely change the role of the Florida state marketing order in the coming years. This issue is discussed more fully in the advertising chapter and the sections on international trade.

First Handler Use of Exchange Mechanisms. Although nonpriced fruit has been the most popular in recent years, contract fruit increased significantly in 1977–78 when there was a short crop because of the 1977 freeze (Table 3.3). Producers were anxious to secure a higher price on the market than they were likely to get in a participation plan. Firms were anxious to secure more fruit and did so by buying through contracts on the spot market. The trend has been upward since 1977–78, which is likely due to freezes experienced in Florida. Participation plans have dropped to a low of 9.5 percent in 1986–87 after a high of 49.5 percent in 1972–73.

A producer selling nonpriced citrus is assured of a market and an average price. With priced citrus the producer is concerned with locating a buyer and determining the best price available when the citrus is ready

Table 3.3. Proportion of Florida citrus sold to processors through various coordinating instruments, 1970-71 through 1986-87.

	Priced citrus		Nonpriced citrus	
Year	Spot	Contract	Contracts (largely participation plan)	Cooperatives and processor owned
1970-71	4.1	14.9	47.3	33.7
1971-72	5.7	16.5	43.7	34.1
1972-73	4.7	12.9	49.5	32.9
1973-74	5.7	13.7	29.9	50.7
1974-75	5.4	14.3	30.0	50.3
1975-76	4.4	18.4	29.1	48.1
1976-77	3.5	14.2	28.7	53.6
1977-78	4.7	25.6	17.3	52.4
1978-79	4.1	28.2	16.3	51.4
1979-80	4.1	25.1	18.4	52.4
1980-81	4.6	25.8	16.5	53.1
1981-82	4.9	25.9	15.4	53.8
1982-83	5.0	30.4	17.7	46.9
1983-84	5.5	33.5	14.0	47.0
1984-85	5.2	43.1	14.2	37.5
1985-86	3.5	34.9	14.1	47.5
1986-87	4.5	41.3	9.5	44.7

Source: Florida Canners Association, various issues (a).

for market (transaction costs). The likelihood of a producer's receiving the season's average price is extremely remote. To improve the likelihood of receiving a price above the average requires an investment of time (transaction costs) devoted to gathering relevant information upon which to base a market decision.

Packer and Processor Exchange Mechanisms. For the most part, the coordinating linkage is direct rather than through auctions. Two important coordinating mechanisms between the processor and buyer are central selling and nonprice contracting with large chains. Statistics are not available on central selling and nonprice contracting. The central seller simply performs the marketing and pricing functions that were historically handled by each processor. Beyond those pooling the marketing functions of a number of processors, the coordination with the central exchange differs little from that of a processor selling direct.

A common practice among many processors and retail chains is to establish verbal contracts to purchase a fixed supply of private label citrus over a season. Processors then have some lead time for the labeling of cans to be shipped to the buyers. However, once the cans have been labeled with specific private labels, individual processors have actually reduced the number of potential buyers for that specific product. Since the product has been labeled but not priced to the buyer, it is not clear whether this coordinating mechanism gives the buyer increased market power.

At the wholesale or f.o.b. market level, a coordinating mechanism often exists between buyers and sellers which allows wholesale buyers, after announcement of an f.o.b. price increase, to purchase given amounts of a product for a specified period of time at the previous or lower price. This procedure is referred to as a buy-in privilege or policy. The amount of product a wholesale buyer may purchase at the lower price depends on the buyer's recent purchase record. The more product a firm has recently purchased the greater the amount of product that may be bought at the lower price. Although buy-in periods in the f.o.b. market for frozen concentrate vary in length, an average buy-in period usually continues for two weeks following the announcement of an f.o.b. price increase. The use of buy-in policies will differ each season depending on the stock levels and the strength of demand.

Buy-in privileges constitute standard methods of operation for most firms purchasing processed citrus products. Buy-in policies allow firms to plan ahead with respect to advertising campaigns, pricing decisions, special promotions, and inventory management.

Coordination of packers with retailers and other buyers depends primarily on the size of the packing operation. Brokers play a major role in coordinating packers and retail buyers. Yet, direct sales through packers with substantial sales forces are important. This is especially true for the Sunkist organization as well as the central sales cooperative (Sealdsweet) in Florida. Few long-term contractual arrangements between packers and retail buyers exist. Published data on the volume sold direct versus the volume sold through brokers is not available.

Trade Organizations. There are no organizations of significance that directly represent a bargaining agent for producers except for the role provided by the cooperative organizations. Trade associations, while not involved in bargaining, are an extremely important structure within the industry. Most Florida producers are members of Florida Citrus Mutual, a producer trade association. This is a powerful organization providing leadership in all phases of the industry. While this organization does not buy or sell products, it does provide market information to growers and reflects the grower point of view in all policies having an impact on Florida citrus.

The Florida Canners Association is a strong trade association and often works jointly with other agencies to solve major industry regulatory and marketing problems. Usually, the Florida Department of Citrus provides the mode or clearinghouse for addressing the various issues and coordinating the input from various trade associations.

Trade associations are less powerful in the other producing states, primarily because Texas packers and processors are much more independent, while California is dominated by one large cooperative. In general, trade associations are an integral part of the citrus industry, and they provide significant coordination functions, especially through their various informational publications. Their role in the political arena is unquestionably essential as the citrus industry continues to expand its world markets and face new competitors.

Other Coordinating Dimensions

The wholesale or f.o.b. price for frozen concentrated orange juice is the major coordinating element within the citrus industry, especially for Florida. If processed product movement is slow with inventories accumulating or if distribution of market shares among the larger processors is different from the norm, then wholesale prices are frequently adjusted. Similarly, product shortages lead to f.o.b. price changes. While the industry generally has a feel for those pressures building up to f.o.b. price changes, the actual price adjustments are announced by one or more processors independently through the issuance of revised price cards. These price cards quote the basic wholesale prices for most processed products in different container sizes and pack. Also, specific product terms, buy-in policies, or trade deals are usually listed with these cards.

The final f.o.b. price ultimately depends on product sales and inventory levels. Prices will be adjusted upward if product sales are strong and if year-ending inventories are projected to be low or downward in case of weak sales and/or projected excess stocks. Infrequently, retaliatory pricing has occurred, but as a rule the f.o.b. price has been an acceptable coordinating tool. In recent seasons the substantial increase in imports has impacted as well as confounded the pricing procedures.

While the f.o.b. orange concentrate price is the major coordinating tool, the unpublished bulk orange concentrate price plays a unique coordinating role in the processor phase of the industry. Bulk concentrate is used for a number of products and quality specifications differ—those for concentrate used in manufacturing are considerably more varied than those for packaged orange juices. The industry has been reluctant to publish a price card on bulk concentrate, since there can be a wide range of specifications. The f.o.b. price for concentrate changes in response to major fundamental conditions in both the United States and Brazil. Frequently, the bulk concentrate price and a derived price for an equivalent quantity of containerized concentrate may differ. If inventories are accumulating at an excessive rate and/or there is considerable uncertainty about Brazilian conditions, the bulk price may be discounted to the f.o.b. card price expressed in equivalent bulk concentrate. This represents a mechanism for moving product in and out of storage.

Timely and accurate data are essential to the economic performance of the citrus industry. Product movement and production statistics are well documented for each producing area with weekly published statistics. The following list, although not exhaustive, identifies the more important weekly statistical reports within the industry:

1. Citrus Administrative Committee—*Disposition of All Certified Florida Citrus*
2. California-Arizona Navel Orange Administrative Committee—*Navel Orange Shipments and Utilization*
3. Texas Valley Citrus Committee—*Fresh Fruit Utilization Report*
4. Florida Canners Association—*Orange Utilization, Prices and Yields*
5. Florida Canners Association—*Carryover, Pack, Movements, and Goods on Hand*
6. Florida Department of Citrus—*Frozen Concentrate and Chilled Orange Juice National Consumer Purchasers*
7. Citrus Associates of the N.Y. Cotton Exchange—*FCOJ Exchange Report*

Within the series of publications, data on weekly product flow are available. This information flows freely throughout the vertical market system and is summarized in a number of different publications. The citrus industry provides a wealth of data, as previously described, through the federal reporting services, trade associations, and other industry organizations. Crop forecasting and demand projection are utilized extensively within the citrus industry. Strong financial support for economic research provides the methodology for demand projections and ultimately economic outlook reports. Similarly, the Crop and Livestock Reporting Service provides a monthly crop estimate (total boxes and yield) for the duration of the citrus harvesting season. These data are used to generate both long-term and short-term crop forecasts.

Most of these research efforts relate to the total industry and not to specific firms. Hence, the research generally has its greatest usefulness in providing economic impact studies for various pricing and inventory policies, as illustrated with the example in Table 3.4. Also, much of the work assists the industry with the evaluation of various advertising programs and other promotional efforts.

Table 3.4. Estimated FCOJ availability, movement, and carryover, Florida 1986-87 season.

	Season average f.o.b. card price ($/dozen 6 ounce cans)		
Item	$3.81	$4.06	$4.31
Availability	Million gallons 42° brix		
Beginning inventory	40.3	40.3	40.3
Pack[a]	150.8	150.8	150.8
Imports[b]	78.0	76.0	73.0
Total	269.1	267.1	264.1
Movement			
Retail	95.0[c]	93.0[d]	90.5[e]
Bulk[f]	115.0	114.3	113.5
Institutional	19.5	19.0	18.6
Total	229.5	226.3	222.6
Carryover	39.6	40.8	41.5
Weeks supply	9.0	9.4	9.7

Source: Brown (1986).
[a]Includes 110.7 million gallons from round oranges and temples and 2.5 million gallons from speciality fruit. Based on yield of 1.33 gallons per box 42° brix.
[b]Foreign and domestic imports plus receipts from non-FCPA members.
[c]Assumes average Nielsen price of 52 per 6 ounce can.
[d]Assumes average Nielsen price of 55 per 6 ounce can.
[e]Assumes average Nielsen price of 58 per 6 ounce can.
[f]Assumes deliveries to the futures market will balance with receipts for the year.

4

•
•
•
•
•
•
•
•
•
•
•
•

Frozen Concentrate Storage Management

Inventory and Risk

Inventory and the USDA Crop Estimate. The harvesting and related marketing activities for U.S. oranges tend to follow an identifiable sequence over time. (See Figure 4.1 for the Florida season.) These events are frequently both forecasted and then monitored after the fact. The first official crop forecast is announced by the USDA in mid-October. Substantial adjustments are generally seen immediately after this first announcement of expected boxes of yield. Variation in either estimated boxes or yield can lead to major adjustments in the expected gallons of juice available. These estimates in conjunction with the accumulated inventories of FCOJ from the crop just harvested represent the first truly quantitative estimate of the total potential supply of juice available for the forthcoming season.

Obviously, the crop estimate may be wrong. Historically, however, the initial estimate has been reasonably accurate in normal years. New estimates are announced monthly (except November) to account for any changes in the crop condition resulting from weather or other major factors influencing supplies. Hurricanes (which in the past have generally had minimal effect on citrus) and freezes both tend to occur when most of the crop has not been harvested. Hence, such natural events can drastically alter the supply picture. Rainfall in previous seasons and the loss of trees resulting from disease and other causes are usually reflected in the October crop estimate. By early June most of the crop is harvested

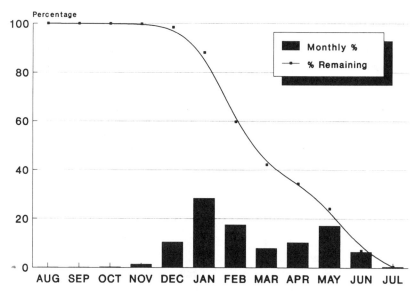

Figure 4.1. Percentage of Florida orange crop remaining to harvest and monthly percentage of total crop harvested, average of 1980–84. *(From Division of Fruit and Vegetable Inspection)*

and the yield known. Seasonal patterns will differ somewhat by domestic regions but overall, those shown in Figure 4.1 are typical.

Within Season Inventory Management. As the crop is harvested, inventories again accumulate. If inventories tend to accumulate faster than the norm, the industry must initiate corrective marketing programs. The citrus industry, under the present market structure, has three major options available to deal with large inventory accumulations. Stepped-up branded and generic advertising programs designed to shift the demand for orange juice may be undertaken. Price cutting at the f.o.b. level can also be used to reduce accumulating inventories. However, because of the inelastic demand for frozen concentrate, this policy also tends to reduce the current season net dollar gain to the industry. Finally, new inventory policies may be implemented, with the amount of FCOJ carried into the next crop year increased. Unlike during the early seventies when Florida processors supplied almost all orange concentrate, processor storage policies must now include an evaluation and speculation about Brazilian supplies. Clearly the value of stored concentrate is directly impacted by Brazilian crop sizes and pricing policies.

Inventory accumulations relative to the expected crop represent a major catalyst for price adjustment. Figure 4.2 shows the typical pattern of inventory accumulations expressed as a percentage of the estimated annual crop as the season progresses. Inventories will continue to accumulate until the harvest season slows to a stop during the summer months. Thus, by monitoring inventories and the crop estimates during a season, one can perhaps detect the degree of price firmness.

The accumulated inventories within the season are usually in bulk form to be used in the later parts of the season to meet product demand. Also, earlier fruit of the new crop year frequently requires blending with other orange juices in order to meet the color and flavor minimums. The industry will try to meet these demands. These ending inventories are usually expressed in terms of weeks of remaining supplies as related to the average weekly movements of concentrate for the year. In more recent seasons these ending inventories have been around 14 weeks. Up until 1970–71 an industry practice of maintaining around 10 weeks of inventories was generally followed. However, as FCOJ annual movements out of Florida continued to increase, processors began carrying proportionally more year-ending stocks (Figure 4.3). This change occurred primarily as a result of leadership from a few dominant processors. Again, availability of imported juices provides a direct alternative

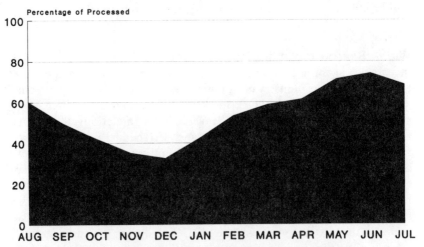

Figure 4.2. Inventory of frozen concentrated orange juice as a percentage of oranges processed annually. *(Calculated from Florida Canners Association and Division of Fruit and Vegetable Inspection)*

to maintaining maximum year-ending stocks. A direct relationship between imports and inventory management has not been measured. Given the processor's desire to always have adequate fruit and juices committed to assure continued plant operations at a reasonable level of efficiency, one would expect the storage patterns illustrated in Figure 4.2 to continue.

The trends in inventory management are shown in Figure 4.3 in which year-ending supplies are related to product movement from 1974–75 through 1983–84 seasons. Ending inventories have increased with greater movements, and the equivalent weeks of ending supplies have trended upward through 1983–84. This upward growth in inventories coordinated with movements suggests that the industry has managed its inventories fairly successfully. However, the level of inventories currently maintained may still not be optimal. Also, in some seasons coordination of inventories becomes especially difficult. In 1976–77, for example, year-ending supplies were substantially below the 14-week norm. Freeze damage reduced supplies, and f.o.b. price increases were inadequate to reduce movements in order to raise inventories to the desired level. Part of the management problem during that season was that f.o.b. prices had more than doubled, and there was reluctance among processors to raise prices further, even with the critical inventory situation. Prices were already in ranges beyond the historical experience of the industry and

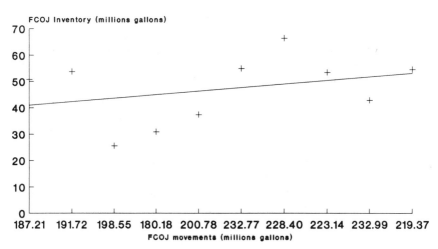

Figure 4.3 Relationship between ending inventories of frozen concentrated orange juice and annual movement out of Florida, 1974–75 through 1983–84. *(From Florida Canners Association)*

this created additional uncertainty as to consumer reactions to further adjustments. Thus, while the industry has historically tried to coordinate inventories, the extreme supply conditions as illustrated with the 1977 season prevented maintaining the level of carryover.

While processors, including cooperatives, currently manage all inventories of processed citrus at the wholesale level, there has been considerable effort to change the current structure. Since much fruit is sold under a nonpricing arrangement through cooperatives or participation plans, the grower loses control over those inventory decisions affecting the returns for fruit. As an alternative, a reserve pool concept has been proposed by Florida producers. Under this plan a share of all fruit (after processing) would be placed in a grower-owned reserve pool. Product would be added to and released from the pool according to specific formulae, and the program would be administered by the Florida Department of Citrus. This program was initially proposed in order to provide an alternative product source to secondary and export markets when wholesale prices were extremely high. These markets would be assured of a continual flow of orange juice at subsidized prices when supplies were short. Of equal importance, however, is the fact that growers would gain some control over those storage decisions that influence the industry. The reserve pool concept received the most interest during periods of "bumper" crops. It has received little interest in the eighties since Florida has experienced substantial crop losses resulting from back-to-back freezes. Likewise, Brazilian juices add another level of risk to lessen the industry's overall ability to manage inventories through the reserve pool arrangement. The industry has historically gone through cycles of interest in developing collective pooling arrangements. As Florida recovers from the losses of the early eighties, the reserve pooling arrangement may once again receive renewed interest.

Finally, large retail food outlets maintain approximately 10 to 14 million gallons of single strength equivalent concentrate in inventories at retail outlets. Between 40 and 50 percent of these inventories are in displays visible to the consumer. Ward (1974) has shown that increases in the visible inventories do increase the consumption of concentrate. Further, retail chains use these inventories to take advantage of special price promotions and buy-in policies at the wholesale level. When actual card prices change, there tends to be substantial buy-in of juice. Likewise, promotions allowing cents off to the retail outlets generally stimulate substantial inventory increases. Retail outlets manage their inventories to take advantage of those specials initiated at the processor level.

In general, the processing phase of the citrus industry has developed considerable management skill with its inventories and the inventories can be viewed as being successfully coordinated with supply and demand conditions. Retail inventory management is insignificant relative to that at the processor level. Finally, a grower control pool, if ever implemented, is not likely to replace a significant part of the storage function currently controlled by processors. All storage policies have become considerably more complex with the growth of imports and the substantial investment in juice-tank farms near major ports out of Florida.

Storage Capacity. The capacity of Florida freezer space usable for storing frozen concentrate is classified as public warehouses versus private and semiprivate. Private warehouses are used primarily to store the processor's stocks of concentrates and other processed citrus products. Public warehouses are those warehouses available for rental on a per unit rate, which is generally quoted in cents per 100 pounds.

The gross Florida freezer space for both public and private ownership is shown in Table 4.1 for the period 1967 through 1983. Usable Florida freezer space has increased. Approximately 55 percent of this space is in public warehouses, while 45 percent is in private. Florida processors generally indicate a preference for maintaining their own storage facilities. Processors tend to store in their own facilities, but public facilities are essential. Public warehouses are available, and these

Table 4.1. Florida gross and usable cold storage freezer space for processed products, 1967 through 1983.

		Percentage of gross freezer	Usable freezer	Total usable space public (private)
		Cu. ft. (millions)	Cu. ft. (millions)	%
Public	1967	28.56	23.73	45.9
	1969	31.51	25.13	43.8
	1971	39.09	32.72	45.8
	1979	73.77	46.29	56.4
	1981	74.32	49.58	55.8
	1983	75.42	54.99	55.2
Private	1967	37.42	28.01	54.2
	1969	40.89	32.22	56.2
	1971	45.66	38.73	54.2
	1979	57.10	33.87	43.6
	1981	58.89	37.26	44.2
	1983	61.11	42.48	44.8

Source: USDA Statistical Reporting Service.

serve as a cushion to handle supplies when crops are extremely large. A combination of available private and public freezer space provides a storage supply in excess of present needs.

Data on total industry storage are not available. Processors have moved to bulk storage in large tanks in conjunction with the traditional drum storage. Large storage facilities in Delaware and California are typical of the trend to develop large storage facilities near consuming centers. Currently, those facilities are used to receive imported concentrate being shipped from Brazil in large tankers.

II

Pricing
and
Risk

5

•
•
•
•
•
•
•
•
•
•
•
•

Product Demand and Prices

Product Substitutability

Product substitution creates an environment of competition among the supplying regions. Generally the California-Arizona orange has an appealing skin appearance and is highly desirable for fresh fruit. The Florida orange has a less appealing outer skin, but the juice content is usually higher than that of the California orange. Therefore, Florida oranges are better suited for processing. The degree of product substitution and price flexibility should differ by region since the products can be differentiated.

F.o.b. price flexibility coefficients for Florida fresh citrus are shown in Table 5.1. These estimates are calculated for 1974–75 and give an approximate indication of product substitutability among fresh supply regions. Considerable substitution is evident for both fresh products. The coefficients for grapefruit indicate little differential between Florida and Texas fresh grapefruit. A study of the world demand for fresh grapefruit further indicates that the domestic f.o.b. grapefruit demand is inelastic, with the elasticity coefficient estimated to be −0.7431 (Ward and Tang 1978). While the total U.S. demand for grapefruit is shown to be inelastic, the high degree of substitutability among regions leads to the more elastic or less flexible demand for Florida grapefruit shown in Table 5.1.

Ward and Tilley (1980) have estimated the retail price elasticities for processed orange products reported in Table 5.2. Using monthly data

63

Table 5.1. F.o.b. price flexibilities for Florida fresh citrus.

Regional supply	Percentage change in Florida's f.o.b. price in response to a 1 percent change in regional supplies	
	Fresh oranges	Fresh grapefruit
Florida	-1.4682	-0.2557
Texas	-0.0322	-0.2364
California	-0.6915	-0.1455

Source: Ward (September 1975).
Note: Flexibility coefficients estimated for 1974-75 based on the shipments for that season.

from 1971 through 1978, the retail elasticity of demand for frozen orange concentrate is estimated to be −1.33 and −0.93 for chilled. Their results show chilled orange juice is substitutable for concentrate, but that statistically, concentrate is not substitutable for chilled juice. This difference in substitutability is partially related to the willingness of consumers to substitute convenience for storability. Chilled juice is in ready-to-consume form, whereas concentrate, while storable over an extended period, must be reconstituted before consumption. Efforts to establish substitution relationships with powders and synthetics have not been successful. Usually synthetics can gain market shares only when citrus prices have risen rapidly such as after a severe freeze. Finally, in a study by Ward (1976, 44), the f.o.b. elasticity for frozen concentrate is shown to be −0.5228 on a quarterly basis.

Estimates of income elasticities from time series data are questionable, since processed citrus consumption has been increasing over time, and only part of the increase is due to income. Hence, most income elasticities are partially distorted, since they often reflect more than just the income effect. Tilley's (1979) estimates of income elasticities were shown to be positive and significant for several citrus products. A cross-

Table 5.2. Retail price elasticities for frozen concentrated orange juice and chilled orange juice, based on monthly consumer panel data through 1979.

Quantity	Percentage change in quantity associated with a 1 percent change in price	
	Frozen concentrated orange juice (FCOJ)	Chilled orange juice (COJ)
FCOJ	-1.33	--
COJ	--	-0.93

Source: Ward and Tilley (1980).

sectional time series study by Ward and Davis (1978) showed a significant positive response between adjacent income groups.

Commodity Price Patterns

All citrus produced in the United States is sold under one of the three alternative pricing plans by growers. First, the fruit may be sold spot to a packinghouse, processor, or middleman (commonly referred to as bird dog). Alternatively, the fruit may be forward priced through either a short- or long-term contract. Under these arrangements the producer knows the selling price before the physical ownership of the fruit has been relinquished. Third, citrus fruit is also sold under a nonpriced arrangement under which each participating producer's fruit is moved into a designated pool shared with other members. The returns to the pool are then determined after the processed or packed product has been sold. Generally these returns and the average prices to the producer are not known until the season ends, at which time each participant receives the average price for the pooled fruit. The pools are usually determined by variety and season and are offered by both private firms and cooperatives.

Retail, f.o.b., delivered-in, and on-tree prices are of particular importance to the citrus industry. For products sold spot the delivered-in price is applicable. If the product is under a pooling arrangement the f.o.b. price less all costs of product transformation is relevant. This latter price is often referred to as the derived delivered-in price, and it may differ from the spot delivered-in price. This difference would reflect in part the gains (or losses) to the producer from selling in a pooling arrangement versus selling in the spot market.

On-tree Prices for Fresh and Processed Citrus. All oranges produced in the United States averaged $3.58 per box (1⅗ bu.) over the period 1971–72 through 1985–86. However, oranges utilized for fresh consumption returned an average on-tree value of $5.18 per box, while processed oranges yielded $3.06 per box. Oranges utilized for fresh consumption consistently sold at a substantial premium over those for processing. Similarly, California on-tree value for fresh oranges consistently exceeded Florida's value, with the average on-tree prices from 1971–72 through 1985–86 being $5.54 and $4.65 respectively (Table 5.3). California generally has the highest fresh fruit price and Texas the lowest, with Florida and Arizona falling in between.

Table 5.3. Season average on-tree price and value of oranges by states, 1971-72 through 1985-86.

Crop year[a]	Price per 1 3/5 bushel box			Value of production ($1,000)		
	Fresh	Processed	Total	Fresh	Processed	Total
			United States			
1971-72	$2.67	$1.75	$1.96	$115,733	$259,373	$375,106
1972-73	3.16	1.36	1.70	133,959	248,325	382,284
1973-74	3.20	1.29	1.69	143,705	221,759	365,464
1974-75	3.04	1.33	1.72	165,171	243,774	408,945
1975-76	2.74	1.51	1.77	137,694	290,796	428,490
1976-77	3.29	1.96	2.21	155,243	383,324	538,567
1977-78	5.98	3.76	4.21	266,697	659,307	926,004
1978-79	6.69	4.23	4.70	269,176	721,193	990,369
1979-80	3.82	3.33	3.42	208,828	727,797	936,625
1980-81	5.39	3.30	3.75	272,097	645,475	917,572
1981-82	8.18	3.78	4.94	379,921	492,612	872,533
1982-83	4.65	3.98	4.15	275,767	658,804	934,571
1983-84	8.39	4.98	5.95	403,565	604,464	1,008,029
1984-84	10.14	6.19	7.41	496,610	679,374	1,175,984
1985-86	6.32	3.22	4.18	346,618	391,034	737,652
Average	5.18	3.06	3.58	--	--	--
			California			
1971-72	$2.82	$0.10	$1.82	$77,253	$1,557	$78,810
1972-73	4.00	0.02	2.30	96,331	292	96,623
1973-74	3.81	-0.35	2.67	111,615	-3,915	107,700
1974-75	3.50	-0.51	1.07	124,532	-9,944	114,588
1975-76	3.00	-0.42	1.79	102,604	-7,866	94,738
1976-77	3.76	-0.66	2.52	122,480	-8,379	114,101
1977-78	6.72	0.25	4.63	193,592	3,450	197,042
1978-79	7.55	0.36	5.14	187,346	4,475	191,821
1979-80	3.74	-0.10	2.45	147,608	-1,996	145,612
1980-81	5.46	-0.28	3.03	205,507	-7,710	197,797
1981-82	9.10	-0.59	7.13	303,792	-5,000	298,792
1982-83	4.37	-0.16	2.42	189,097	-5,186	183,911
1983-84	8.37	-0.90	6.55	327,701	-9,886	317,815
1984-85	10.01	1.23	8.00	404,262	14,724	418,986
1985-86	6.49	-1.29	4.93	284,132	-14,190	269,942
Average	5.54	-.22	3.76	--	--	--
			Florida			
1971-72	$2.50	$2.01	$2.04	$28,134	$252,183	$280,317
1972-73	1.85	1.54	1.56	22,645	242,716	265,361
1973-74	2.10	1.43	1.47	23,293	221,398	244,691
1974-75	2.11	1.58	1.62	28,196	252,154	280,350
1975-76	2.25	1.74	1.77	26,392	295,057	321,449
1976-77	2.20	2.17	2.17	19,593	386,389	405,982
1977-78	4.85	4.09	4.14	48,373	645,304	693,677
1978-79	5.36	4.61	4.66	62,727	702,234	764,961
1979-80	4.16	3.70	3.72	45,720	723,157	768,877
1980-81	5.79	3.96	4.04	47,927	649,304	697,231
1981-82	6.51	4.14	4.28	49,621	489,065	538,686
1982-83	5.94	5.08	5.15	61,273	657,147	718,420

Table 5.3. (continued).

Crop year[a]	Price per 1 3/5 bushel box			Value of production ($1,000)		
	Fresh	Processed	Total	Fresh	Processed	Total
1983-84	7.75	5.61	5.75	59,245	611,373	670,618
1984-85	11.11	6.83	7.10	73,911	664,012	737,923
1985-86	5.34	3.68	3.81	47,446	405,636	453,082
Average	4.65	3.48	3.55	--	--	--

Texas

1971-72	$1.73	$1.37	$1.53	$4,758	$4,658	$9,416
1972-73	1.34	0.99	1.13	4,295	4,549	8,844
1973-74	1.28	1.04	1.13	3,072	4,368	7,440
1974-75	1.87	1.00	1.46	4,507	2,130	6,637
1975-76	1.61	1.28	1.45	4,959	3,866	8,825
1976-77	2.06	1.72	1.89	7,025	6,003	13,028
1977-78	3.33	3.41	3.37	10,556	9,991	20,547
1978-79	3.88	3.09	3.35	8,148	13,287	21,435
1979-80	4.67	3.29	4.00	9,714	6,415	16,129
1980-81	4.13	3.07	3.76	11,758	4,537	16,295
1981-82	4.01	3.28	3.69	13,320	8,595	21,915
1982-83	4.16	2.93	3.65	13,894	6,856	20,750
1983-84	4.10	2.70	3.48	5,699	3,024	8,723
1984-85	0	0	0	0	0	0
1985-86	9.29	4.01	8.95	2,694	80	2,774
Average	3.39	2.37	3.06	--	--	--

Arizona

1971-72	$2.75	$0.34	$1.34	$ 5,588	$975	$6,563
1972-73	3.73	0.35	2.27	10,688	768	11,456
1973-74	2.73	-0.07	1.66	5,725	-92	5,633
1974-75	3.69	-0.2	81.49	7,936	-566	7,370
1975-76	3.04	-0.18	1.30	3,739	-261	3,478
1976-77	2.66	-0.42	1.38	6,145	-689	5,456
1977-78	5.38	0.57	4.07	14,176	562	14,738
1978-79	6.68	0.95	4.19	10,955	1,197	12,152
1979-80	2.63	0.17	1.71	5,786	221	6,007
1980-81	4.11	-0.71	2.41	6,905	-656	6,249
1981-82	6.22	-0.05	4.31	13,188	-481	3,140
1982-83	4.52	-0.01	3.02	11,503	-131	1,490
1983-84	7.23	-0.16	6.04	10,920	-47	10,873
1984-85	9.55	1.23	7.79	18,437	638	19,075
1985-86	6.64	-1.12	5.15	12,346	-492	11,854
Average	4.77	0.04	3.21	--	--	--

Source: Florida Crop and Livestock Reporting Service, various issues.
[a]September 1 through August 31.

All grapefruit produced in the United States averaged $2.37 per box (1⅗ bu.) from 1971-72 through 1985-86. Grapefruit utilized for fresh consumption average 2.7 times more per box ($3.67) than grapefruit used for processing ($1.36). California generally has the highest fresh price ($4.81 per box), with Florida ($3.66), Arizona ($3.53), and Texas ($2.74) experiencing a lower price per box. For processed grapefruit Florida generally has the higher price per box ($1.64), followed by Texas ($1.12), Arizona ($-0.46), and California ($-0.50). In all producing areas the on-tree returns from processed grapefruit were substantially below those from fresh sales and were actually negative in California and Arizona (Tables 5.4).

Table 5.4. Season average on-tree price and value of grapefruit by states, 1971-72 through 1985-86.

Crop year[a]	Price per 1 3/5 bushel box			Value of production ($1,000)		
	Fresh	Processed	Total	Fresh	Processed	Total
			United States			
1971-72	$3.04	$1.63	$2.23	$82,134	$60,895	$143,029
1972-73	2.96	1.29	1.98	81,150	49,187	130,337
1973-74	2.48	0.97	1.61	68,636	36,631	105,267
1974-75	2.96	0.66	1.72	83,943	21,482	105,425
1975-76	2.31	0.61	1.40	75,198	22,976	98,174
1976-77	2.47	0.88	1.49	70,477	40,799	111,276
1977-78	2.46	0.93	1.55	74,228	41,572	115,800
1978-79	3.53	1.48	2.35	100,470	57,453	157,923
1979-80	4.04	2.35	3.01	114,536	105,208	219,744
1980-81	5.15	2.36	3.50	143,221	94,341	237,562
1981-82	3.94	0.66	1.99	113,282	27,434	140,716
1982-83	3.18	0.22	1.79	102,169	6,303	108,472
1983-84	4.19	1.30	2.68	107,629	36,236	143,865
1984-85	6.39	2.31	4.01	147,888	75,593	223,481
1985-86	5.92	2.69	4.21	161,507	81,931	243,438
Average	3.67	1.36	2.37	--	--	--
			California			
1971-72	$4.27	$0.34	$2.42	$12,426	$884	$13,310
1972-73	3.78	0.14	1.95	10,866	409	11,295
1973-74	3.37	0.22	1.87	8,189	488	8,677
1974-75	3.19	-0.12	1.60	11,356	-406	10,950
1975-76	2.63	-0.11	1.27	9,547	-393	9,154
1976-77	2.90	-0.49	1.38	12,325	-1,690	10,635
1977-78	4.80	-0.66	2.24	21,312	-2,596	18,716
1978-79	6.59	-0.67	3.70	24,317	-1,635	22,682
1979-80	4.50	-0.48	1.82	15,570	-1,939	13,631
1980-81	6.34	-0.45	3.33	28,465	-1,615	26,850
1981-82	3.95	-1.31	1.85	14,635	-3,203	11,432
1982-83	4.05	-1.31	1.94	17,901	-3,773	14,128
1983-84	5.30	-1.53	2.83	24,469	-4,008	20,461
1984-85	8.18	-0.44	5.63	50,732	-1,156	49,576
1985-86	8.35	-0.58	5.69	49,272	-1,462	47,810
Average	4.81	-0.50	2.63	--	--	--

Table 5.4. (continued).

Crop year[a]	Price per 1 3/5 bushel box			Value of production ($1,000)		
	Fresh	Processed	Total	Fresh	Processed	Total

Florida

1971-72	$3.14	$1.85	$2.32	$53,453	$55,538	$108,991
1972-73	3.10	1.47	2.08	52,910	41,725	94,635
1973-74	2.54	1.10	1.66	47,478	32,401	79,879
1974-75	3.03	0.76	1.72	57,003	19,364	76,367
1975-76	2.48	0.75	1.47	50,651	21,504	72,155
1976-77	2.60	1.10	1.58	42,382	38,734	81,116
1977-78	2.35	1.26	1.64	42,224	42,214	84,438
1978-79	3.23	1.87	2.41	63,596	56,532	120,128
1979-80	4.15	2.85	3.31	80,422	100,786	181,208
1980-81	5.25	2.76	3.60	89,695	91,460	181,155
1981-82	4.48	0.82	2.09	74,846	25,751	100,597
1982-83	3.61	0.52	1.96	66,195	11,026	77,221
1983-84	4.20	1.70	2.72	69,894	41,264	111,158
1984-85	5.62	2.66	3.67	84,208	77,148	161,356
1985-86	5.19	3.09	3.97	101,732	83.890	185,622
Average	3.66	1.64	2.41	--	--	--

Arizona

1971-72	$2.65	$0.20	$1.44	$3,397	$252	$3,649
1972-73	2.40	0.30	1.22	2,772	446	3,218
1973-74	2.30	0.15	1.34	2,601	138	2,739
1974-75	2.70	0.10	1.40	3,726	139	3,865
1975-76	1.90	-0.05	0.76	2,423	-90	2,333
1976-77	2.50	-0.40	0.99	3,588	-626	2,962
1977-78	2.20	-0.74	0.44	2,640	-1,332	1,308
1978-79	4.34	-0.62	1.69	4,557	-744	3,813
1979-80	3.93	-0.42	1.49	5,188	-706	4,482
1980-81	4.91	-0.20	2.72	7,856	-240	7,616
1981-82	3.66	-1.28	1.01	4,063	-1,651	2,412
1982-83	2.73	-1.32	1.11	4,423	-1,426	2,997
1983-84	4.44	-1.52	2.54	6,860	-1,102	5,758
1984-85	6.64	-0.38	4.18	12,948	-399	12,549
1985-86	5.66	-0.66	3.40	8,717	-568	8,149
Average	3.53	-0.46	1.72	--	--	--

Texas

1971-72	$2.24	$1.22	$1.86	$12,858	$4,221	$17,079
1972-73	2.30	1.21	1.80	14,582	6,607	21,189
1973-74	1.92	0.68	1.31	10,368	3,604	13,972
1974-75	2.55	0.90	1.95	11,858	2,385	14,243
1975-76	1.73	0.57	1.36	12,577	1,955	14,532
1976-77	1.88	0.74	1.34	12,182	4,381	16,563
1977-78	1.22	0.62	0.95	8,052	3,286	11,338
1978-79	2.00	0.66	1.26	8,000	3,300	11,300
1979-80	3.18	1.91	2.59	13,356	7,067	20,423
1980-81	3.70	2.31	3.27	17,205	4,736	21,941
1981-82	2.73	0.98	1.89	19,738	6,537	26,275
1982-83	1.75	0.14	1.26	13,650	476	14,126
1983-84	2.24	0.24	2.03	6,406	82	6,488
1984-85	0	0	0	0	0	0
1985-86	8.93	3.53	8.44	1,786	71	1,857
Average	2.74	1.12	2.24	--	--	--

Source: Florida Crop and Livestock Reporting Service, various issues.
[a]September 1 through August 31.

Fresh and Processed Citrus Prices. The absolute price margin for fresh California oranges exceeds Florida's price margin except during the last two years. Between 1972–73 and 1985–86 Florida's on-tree price as a percentage of the f.o.b. price was 48.1 percent while California's was 50.3 percent (Table 5.5). This indicates that California's farmers receive a slightly higher percentage of the f.o.b. price than Florida's farmers as well as a larger absolute amount. Florida growers received an on-tree value that was 44 percent of the f.o.b. value of oranges used in processed products (Table 5.6), which is slightly less than for oranges sold fresh.

Prices in the processing phase of the citrus industry differ substantially from those of the fresh market. Likewise, the unit of measurement differs. Prices are measured in dollars per pounds of solids or some conversion thereof. Since the conversion from boxes to processed juice depends on the juice yield per box, it is less meaningful to discuss in terms of boxes.

Table 5.5. Comparison of f.o.b. and on-tree prices for Florida and California fresh oranges in 90 pound box equivalents, 1972-73 through 1985-86.

Crop year[c]	FLORIDA			CALIFORNIA		
	On-tree[a]	F.o.b.[b]	Margins	On-tree[a]	F.o.b.[b]	Margins
1972-73	$1.85 (40)[d]	4.66	2.81	$4.00 (48)[d]	8.33	4.33
1973-74	2.10 (41)	5.16	3.06	3.81 (44)	8.62	4.81
1974-75	2.11 (40)	5.30	3.19	3.50 (40)	8.68	5.18
1975-76	2.25 (40)	5.69	3.44	3.00 (36)	8.26	5.26
1976-77	2.20 (37)	5.93	3.73	3.76 (42)	9.04	5.28
1977-78	4.85 (54)	8.99	4.14	6.72 (53)	12.60	5.88
1978-79	5.36 (53)	10.17	4.81	7.55 (45)	16.79	9.24
1979-80	4.16 (49)	8.46	4.30	3.74 (33)	11.34	7.60
1980-81	5.79 (52)	11.11	5.32	5.46 (43)	12.72	7.26
1981-82	6.51 (54)	11.95	5.44	9.10 (52)	17.55	8.45
1982-83	5.94 (50)	11.85	5.91	4.37 (35)	12.48	8.11
1983-84	7.75 (56)	13.92	6.17	8.73 (51)	17.28	8.55
1984-85	11.11 (63)	17.74	6.63	10.01 (102)	9.86	-.15
1985-86	5.34 (44)	12.20	6.86	6.49 (80)	8.14	1.65

[a]Florida Crop and Livestock Reporting Service, various issues.
[b]Florida Citrus Mutual, various issues.
[c]September 1 through August 31.
[d]On-tree price as a percentage of f.o.b. price.

Table 5.6. Average season price for Florida oranges used in frozen concentrate, 1966-67 through 1985-86.

Crop year[e]	On-tree[a]	Delivered-in[b]	F.o.b.[c]	Retail[d]	F.o.b.-delivered-in margin	Retail-F.o.b. margin
		Dollars per pound solids				
1966-67	0.16 (66)[f]	0.21	0.47[b]	0.69	0.26 (124)[g]	0.22 (47)[h]
1967-68	0.32 (50)	0.46	0.64[b]	0.83	0.18 (39)	0.19 (30)
1968-69	0.32 (54)	0.53	0.70[b]	0.95	0.17 (32)	0.25 (36)
1969-70	0.20 (66)	0.35	0.58[b]	0.87	0.23 (66)	0.29 (50)
1970-71	0.24 (62)	0.37	0.63[b]	0.88	0.26 (70)	0.25 (40)
1971-72	0.35 (53)	0.50	0.74[b]	0.97	0.24 (48)	0.23 (31)
1972-73	0.26 (62)	0.40	0.68	0.94	0.29 (73)	0.26 (38)
1973-74	0.21 (71)	0.43	0.72	0.96	0.28 (65)	0.24 (33)
1974-75	0.27 (66)	0.41	0.80	1.03	0.39 (95)	0.23 (29)
1975-76	0.30 (63)	0.53	0.80	1.04	0.27 (51)	0.24 (30)
1976-77	0.45 (55)	0.50	1.01	1.26	0.51 (102)	0.25 (25)
1977-78	0.74 (44)	0.95	1.31	1.69	0.36 (38)	0.38 (29)
1978-79	0.76 (45)	1.06	1.38	1.81	0.32 (30)	0.43 (31)
1979-80	0.62 (49)	0.85	1.22	1.63	0.37 (44)	0.41 (34)
1980-81	0.76 (53)	1.06	1.60	2.10	0.54 (51)	0.50 (31)
1981-82	0.78 (54)	1.22	1.71	2.27	0.49 (40)	0.56 (33)
1982-83	0.83 (51)	1.14	1.69	2.20	0.55 (48)	0.51 (30)
1983-84	1.04 (50)	1.24	2.09	2.51	0.85 (69)	0.42 (20)
1984-85	1.19 (44)	1.69	2.16	2.69	0.47 (28)	0.53 (25)
1985-86	0.64 (62)	0.98	1.69	2.36	0.71 (72)	0.67 (40)
C V[i]	58%	54%	47%	45%		

[a]Calculated from Florida Crop and Livestock Reporting Service, various issues.
[b]Florida Citrus Mutual, various issues.
[c]Calculated from Brooks.
[d]Calculated from Table 5.7 and Brooks.
[e]September 1 through August 31.
[f]On-tree to f.o.b. price margin as a percentage of f.o.b. price.
[g]F.o.b. to delivered-in price margin as a percentage of delivered-in price.
[h]Retail to f.o.b. price margin as a percentage of f.o.b. price.
[i]Coefficient of variation.

Florida statistics provide the most detailed information on processing prices; hence, these statistics are used to illustrate the pricing patterns. At the outset Florida on-tree returns for processed oranges and grapefruit consistently exceeded those of other producing areas (Table 5.3 and 5.4). In fact, negative on-tree returns have been recorded for California and Arizona processed citrus during a number of seasons.

The price patterns of frozen concentrated orange juice are generally representative of all citrus processed products. Table 5.6 includes the prices of oranges used in frozen concentrate at each stage of production and distribution. Considerable seasonal variation in prices occurs over time. The adjustments can usually be related to the actual and projected availability of concentrate. Comparing the prices before and after processing shows that price variability (coefficient of variation) to the growers is higher than the price variability at other levels of the vertical system (Table 5.6). In fact, price variability declines as the FCOJ moves closer to the consumer.

The on-tree and delivered-in prices include juice that has been sold to the processor as priced and nonpriced. In seasons of shortages noncommitted citrus usually sells at a premium, and this tends to raise the delivered-in average price. In seasons of excess there is less processor demand for the noncommitted fruit, and the spot price generally becomes depressed. These adjustments tend to produce greater variation in delivered-in prices.

The actual price spreads for each season since 1966–67 are given in Table 5.6. The spreads between the delivered-in and f.o.b. and the f.o.b.-retail prices are similar in magnitude. The f.o.b.-delivered-in margin averaged $.387 per pound solid over 20 years. The retail-f.o.b. margin averaged $.353 per pound solid over 20 years (Table 5.6). This indicates that approximately equal value is added at the processing level and at points between the processor and the consumer. However, the f.o.b.-retail spread averaged 33 percent of the f.o.b. price over the last 20 seasons, whereas the delivered-in-f.o.b. spread averaged 59 percent of the delivered-in value over the last 20 seasons (Table 5.6). Thus, even though equal values are added, the percentage markups vary by a large amount.

Retail prices for the three major processed orange juice products are listed in Table 5.7. Both chilled and canned orange juice consistently sold at a premium in comparison to an equivalent quantity of frozen concentrate. Between 1971 and 1979 the price of chilled orange juice was generally higher than canned juice. Since 1979 canned single strength orange juice has had the higher price, which suggests that they are reaching

Table 5.7. Retail processed citrus prices 1971 through 1986.

Year	Frozen concentrated orange juice	Chilled orange juice	Canned single strength orange juice
	Dollars per single strength equivalent gallon		
1971[a]	1.00	1.56	1.24
1972[a]	1.10	1.59	1.33
1973[a]	1.06	1.55	1.31
1974[a]	1.09	1.52	1.38
1975[a]	1.16	1.53	1.52
1976[a]	1.18	1.60	1.64
1977[b]	1.34	1.72	1.71
1978[b]	1.91	2.28	1.96
1979[b]	2.05	2.62	2.46
1980[b]	1.84	2.16	2.54
1981[b]	2.27	2.60	3.06
1982[b]	2.36	2.64	3.35
1983[b]	2.29	2.56	3.43
1984[b]	2.61	2.79	4.12
1985[b]	2.80	3.07	4.34
1986[b]	2.46	2.62	4.12

Source: [a]Florida Citrus Mutual, various issues.
[b]Florida Department of Citrus, Economic and Market Research Department, various issues.

different markets. This observation is consistent with the demand studies which showed only a weak degree of substitutability between chilled and canned.

Meeting Consumer Demand Preferences

Both economic and marketing research are an integral part of the citrus industry. These research programs have the specific mandates to develop an understanding of the responsiveness of consumers to economic factors and to analyze the demographics and preference of consumers. Advertising research is of particular interest to both research programs. Both research arms are constantly monitoring A.C. Nielsen Co. data and data from NPD Group Marketing and Research Companies in an attempt to detect changes in consumer demand. Florida also maintains a field staff throughout the United States with the partial duty of gathering information about consumer preferences. However, the staff has been significantly reduced in size in the last several seasons.

To the extent that the changes in consumer preferences are for a different form, place, and time of delivery of the product, the resources of the citrus industry are extremely flexible. Different blends and citrus product types can readily be produced. Different packs such as concentrate, chilled, or canned juices in a number of container sizes have evolved in response to changing consumer preferences. Response to consumer preference for away-from-home consumption is reflected in the growth of institutional packages. These packages are in individual servings as well as larger units in order to secure the wide variety of institutional demands.

Consumer preferences are of the utmost importance to the industry. Orange products are not highly differentiated in terms of quality, yet branded substitutes are in the market striving for an increased market share. Considerable promotional efforts have recently been designed to stimulate additional citrus juice consumption for other than breakfast markets.

Pricing Patterns

Fresh Citrus Prices. Fresh citrus retail prices have generally trended upward since 1970–71. This general trend is also seen in the f.o.b. prices of all states except California, where f.o.b. prices were generally stable from 1972–73 through 1975–76 for oranges. The large differential between retail and f.o.b. prices generally reflects a bulky product that requires special handling, and spoilage is a very real factor. Transportation costs from the West Coast to the East Coast and from mid-Florida to New York City increase the differential. The differential between the retail orange prices of California and Florida represents consumer preference for fresh California oranges, higher growing and packing costs in California, and higher transportation costs per box of citrus (Figures 5.1.a. and 5.1.b.).

The f.o.b. and on-tree returns tend to be highly correlated in all states. On-tree returns in California for fresh oranges and grapefruit were steady to downward in trend from 1970–71 through 1975–76 and then started to trend upward in 1976–77. A mixed but steady trend is seen in Texas and Florida for grapefruit and oranges from 1970–71 through 1976–77 with a mixed upward trend starting in 1977–78. In general, the grove owner is the residual income claimant in the vertical market chain. If prices are high at the consumer level, on-tree returns are enhanced. A series of freezes in Florida starting in January of 1977 and occurring again in 1981, 1982, 1983, and 1985 have shortened supplies and increased on-tree returns.

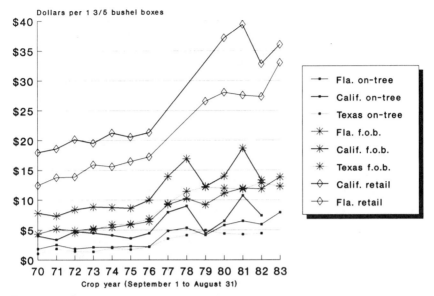

Figure 5.1.a. On-tree, f.o.b., and retail prices of fresh oranges by state. *(From Sunkist Growers, Growers Administrative Committee, and Florida Crop and Livestock Reporting Service)*

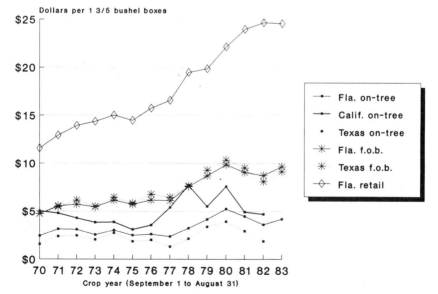

Figure 5.1.b. On-tree, f.o.b., and retail prices of fresh grapefruit by state. *(From Sunkist Growers, Growers Administrative Committee, and Florida Crop and Livestock Reporting Service)*

F.O.B. Frozen Concentrated Orange Juice Price. The f.o.b. price of frozen concentrated orange juice has been shown to be the focal point of the citrus industry. All pricing issues and series obviously cannot be adequately discussed in one chapter. Therefore, the discussion will be limited to current pricing practices having the most economic significance.

Ultimately the behavior among processors and the overall performance of the citrus industry hinges on how well f.o.b. prices for concentrate reflect the supply and demand conditions of the industry. This f.o.b. price can be classified as administered by individual processors. However, the discretionary latitude of any one processor is limited by the number of closely related competitors as well as by the buildup of inventories. Grower pressures, generally against price cuts, present the processor with an incentive against price concessions off the card price, while retail buyers exert the opposite influence on the processor. Inventory accumulations present the processor with a major force when setting pricing policies. Prices will also vary among processors, depending on the extent of product differentiation. Price premiums are evident with brands heavily backed by large advertising programs; hence the latitude in administered pricing under these circumstances is broader.

The historical adjustments in the f.o.b. price for frozen concentrated orange juice are shown in Figure 5.2. In the early seventies the price remained highly stable, with coefficients of variations between 0 and .09 for price changes within each season. These seasons generally reflected a period of growth in both supply and demand. During seasons 1967, 1971, 1977, 1981, 1982, and 1983 the Florida citrus industry experienced freezes causing considerable price adjustments. Of particular significance was the price adjustment in early 1977, 1981, and 1983 following a severe freeze. While processors responded to changing supply conditions, considerable market uncertainty prevailed because prices were raised far above historical levels. Furthermore, in the 1980s a substantial rise in imports greatly impacted the pricing structure for processed citrus. (See Chapter 9.)

Figure 5.3 shows the prices of processed oranges at each major marketing level in the industry. In general, these prices are related throughout the vertical market system. Overall, delivered-in returns did not greatly differ according to product use until 1980–81 (Figure 5.4). This is likely due to the freezes that occurred in Florida.

Figure 5.2. Florida frozen concentrated, orange juice f.o.b. price changes, 1969 through 1984. *(From Florida Citrus Mutual)*

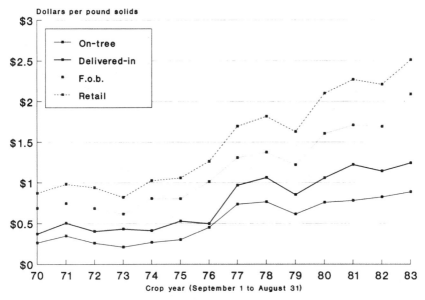

Figure 5.3. Seasonal average prices of Florida frozen concentrated orange juice at different marketing levels. *(From Florida Crop and Livestock Reporting Service and Florida Department of Citrus)*

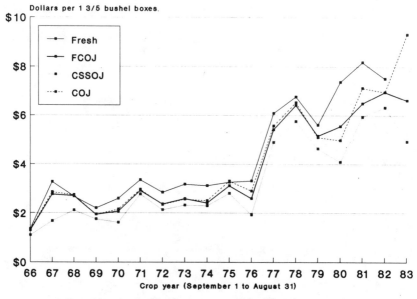

Figure 5.4. Delivered-in price for Florida oranges used in different processed products. *(From Florida Citrus Mutual)*

Industry Price Adjustment to Freezes.

In reviewing the price adjustments noted in Figure 5.3 it is evident that freezes cause major price movements. The price reported (i.e., card price) from which the derived price is calculated is generally increased immediately after the freeze. Additional price increases follow in the subsequent months as information on the product availability and movements change. The spot price generally does not increase immediately after the freeze and tends to lag the increases in the f.o.b. card price. In the few weeks immediately after the freeze, processors are primarily trying to utilize as much of the damaged fruit under contract as possible. Hence, there is a momentary decline in spot purchases. Also, there is concern over the quality of the noncommitted fruit damaged by the freeze. As the season progresses and undamaged noncommitted fruit become available, the spot price increases relative to the derived price.

The retail price, as reported through consumer purchase records, generally shows a corresponding increase. There is generally some lag between the card price change and that price finally paid by the consumer. Nevertheless, a rapid adjustment at the retail level may be evident.

Bulk FCOJ Pricing. The bulk price of frozen concentrated orange juice (FCOJ) is not reported in a periodic report. However, both the f.o.b. and delivered-in prices for retail and institutional packs are reported weekly, and cost data are available on an annual basis. A derived equivalent bulk price can be calculated by using the cost values in conjunction with the weekly price reports. In recent years the bulk price has been more closely attuned to the Brazilian concentrate price. Hence, a derived bulk price using the reported delivered-in and associated processing costs is probably less accurate given the significant increases in imports of concentrate.

Frequently the delivered-in price equivalent to the f.o.b. and the actual delivered-in price differ. This is especially notable during periods of large crops. If the actual delivered-in price is discounted to the derived delivered-in, then the bulk price should lie somewhere between these values when the same cost data are applied to both. The closer the actual price is to the derived delivered-in price, the smaller the possible price range should be in the derivation of the bulk price.

Although the bulk price is not published, samples among processors indicate that the price does vary among processors to a greater degree than do the f.o.b. prices. Much of the price difference can be explained in terms of product form, time of availability, and Brazilian price policies. (See Chapter 10 for a discussion of Brazilian pricing policies.)

Several factors explain bulk price variation among suppliers. The value of bulk juice is an imputed value derived by each supplier. For the processor the imputed value is derived by adding bulk processing cost to the delivered-in price. Cost statistics collected annually suggest that these processing costs and delivered-in prices paid vary among processors. Hence, the imputed value of bulk to each processor may differ. Even though the f.o.b. price reported for FCOJ is fairly constant across processors, at times unpublicized allowances are made which would again change the imputed value of bulk juice to one processor. Also, concentrate sources for some processors may be based totally on the domestic crop while other processors use both domestic and imported juices. Any one processor's quotes for bulk concentrate are obviously tied to the costs of the bulk product, thus giving rise to potential differences in bulk prices among processors. All bulk juice must meet rigid standards; however, quality differences exist, and these must be reflected in the bulk price quoted by a processor. Likewise, other forms of differentiation such as services performed lead to a price difference.

Finally, the imputed value of bulk juices is related to the processor's inventory position and risk acceptance level. In situations of high inventories and high price risk a processor may quote a bulk price less than the full imputed value in an effort to lessen inventory and risk problems. Some juice could be priced to cover only the variable cost of processing if the fixed cost of the operation can be covered through the retail FCOJ packs. Ultimately, a definitive explanation of why bulk values differ cannot be documented in total. Rather, a combination of those factors unique to each supplier leads to some price difference among suppliers.

Over time the bulk price like all citrus prices is subject to uncertainties of supply and demand. Demand changes are relatively stable and predictable. Supplies, however, are subject to considerable variation. Oranges for processing into FCOJ are processed in a concentrated geographic area subject to very similar weather influences. A major freeze can occur in the middle of the harvesting season, leading to large reductions in supplies. The value of bulk FCOJ already processed can change overnight depending upon changes in the raw supply. Part of the pre-freeze value of bulk juice lies in its convenience yield. That is, processors store and value some juice to meet future expected and unexpected demands and part of the price reflects the imputed value for future sales. If a freeze does not occur then the convenience yield of the same juice must decline. Also, the speculative value of carrying inventories prior to the freeze period declines if a freeze does not occur. In essence, the degree of price uncertainty has a weighted influence on the value of bulk juice.

The packing and annual carryover of bulk FCOJ was shown earlier. Total bulk usage falls within five major categories which account for the product at any point in time. Generally, the largest use of domestic bulk concentrate is for reprocessing into retail and institutional packs of concentrate. Reconstitution of domestic bulk juice into chilled orange juices represents the second largest use of bulk concentrate. This form of reprocessing generally takes place within Florida. Most reprocessing of bulk juices out of Florida goes into the production of ready-to-serve orange juice. This latter use parallels the reprocessing of imported bulk concentrate that is predominantly for ready-to-serve markets.

As a general rule, the usage of bulk juices has trended upward. Reprocessing into FCOJ represents a large share of bulk usage, and much of this use of the juice does not require a buyer-seller-type transaction since many domestic processors produce both bulk and retail pack. However, the fact that the bulk operations have grown would suggest that more of the bulk gallons are now traded through cash transactions.

Prices and Product Size. The processing phase of the citrus industry has several types of containers for use in the retail marketing of orange concentrate. The major three containers are the 6-ounce can, the 12-ounce can, and the 16-ounce can. Overall, the f.o.b. price of 6-ounce containers exceeds 12-ounce by roughly 5 percent (Table 5.8). This difference primarily reflects the higher container cost for the smaller cans. The retail price for 12-ounce cans has occasionally exceeded the smaller container price, however. The higher price for 12-ounce sizes, at first glance, suggests that the cost savings from larger containers has not been passed on to the consumers. Studies indicate that large processors with substantial brand distribution may sell larger quantities of the 12-ounce can than other firms. These brands generally sell at a premium price as a result of successful advertising programs. Hence, at least part of the retail price premium for 12-ounce containers may be reflecting brand differentiation.

Pricing Frozen Concentrated Orange Juice Exports. The citrus industry is in a position to both import and export frozen concentrate orange juice. Exports provide the industry with an additional outlet for concentrate; however, imports create considerable controversy as to whether this imported juice is economically desirable for the industry.

Table 5.8. F.o.b. and retail prices for 6 and 12 ounce cans of Florida concentrated orange juice, 1969-70 through 1986-87.

	F.o.b.[a]		Retail[c]	
Season	6 ounce	12 ounce	6 ounce	12 ounce
		$ per case[d]		
1969-70	6.24	5.94	8.89	8.80
1970-71	6.54	6.24	8.86	8.90
1971-72	7.52	7.22	9.85	9.93
1972-73	7.03	6.73	9.57	9.79
1973-74	7.28	6.98	9.76	10.13
1974-75	8.08	7.88[b]	10.37	10.79
1975-76	8.16	7.96[b]	NA	NA
1976-77	10.22	9.96[b]	NA	NA
1977-78	13.28	12.95[b]	17.85[e]	18.00[e]
1978-79	13.96	13.61[b]	18.83[e]	18.79[e]
1979-80	12.35	12.04[b]	17.90[ef]	17.03[ef]
1980-81	15.61	15.22[b]	21.23[e]	20.37[e]
1981-82	15.98	15.57[b]	22.08[e]	20.88[e]
1982-83	15.80	15.41[b]	NA	NA
1983-84	19.51	19.02[b]	NA	NA
1984-85	20.31	19.89[b]	NA	NA
1985-86	15.83	15.41	NA	NA
1986-87	17.48	16.89	NA	NA

[a]F.o.b. prices as quoted on processor's price cards.
[b]Calculated by multiplying the 6 ounce price times .975.
[c]Florida Department of Citrus, Economic and Market Research Department.
[d]A case contains 48 6 ounce or 24 12 ounce cans (288 ounces of concentrate).
[e]NPD Research.
[f]Data available for October and November only.

U.S. concentrate is exported to both Canadian and European markets. The Canadian market differs little from the domestic market. In contrast, the European market is expected to differ substantially from the U.S. market. The citrus industry faces a number of competing suppliers in Europe. Often the foreign concentrate exported to Europe is priced lower than the U.S. export price. Recognizing that competition exists in the European market, how should the United States price its product relative to the world price?

Many processors have argued that a two-pricing system between domestic and exported juice is desirable. Two aspects of international markets allow the two-pricing program to become operational. First, the domestic price has consistently been at a premium relative to the world price. Second, U.S. tariff controls allow 99 percent of all duties on concentrate imports to be regained once an equivalent quantity of concentrate is exported. Thus, imports can be brought into the domestic market if an equivalent quantity is exported. Under these arrangements the differential between domestic and world prices can be used by exporters to average down the European export price. However, in the 1980s imports have been used this way only to a limited extent because it has become more profitable to import the juice and sell in the domestic market.

Demand models developed by Ward were used to compare various differential pricing levels. The result from the models clearly shows that a two-pricing system between the domestic and export market is desirable. Comparing the European and domestic elasticities of demand, the empirical evidence shows that total returns to the citrus industry can be increased by supporting a rise in the domestic price and lowering the export price to Europe. That is, exports to Europe should be discounted to the domestic market in order to increase total revenues (Ward 1976a). One consequence of increased gross revenues through rising domestic prices is inventory accumulations. Discounting the export price from some fixed domestic price will reduce inventories. European exports can absorb part of domestic inventory accumulations; however, the European market alone is too small to reduce inventories to acceptable levels.

The benefits of a two-pricing program will differ according to the method used to sustain the price differential. The differential between the f.o.b. domestic price of concentrate and the equivalent price of Brazilian concentrate has a profound effect on both the total amount of imports brought into Florida and on the export price of concentrate shipped to Europe. For every 1 percent increase in the spread between the domestic price and the price of imports (net of import duties), imports are expected to increase 2.7 percent (Ward 1976a). That is, imports are very elastic with respect to the price spread, and domestic increases will lead to proportionally greater increases in imports. (See Chapter 9 for a detailed discussion of this topic.)

Further, both the domestic and import prices play a direct role in the derivation of the export price to Europe. As a general guideline, the industry's export pricing has been such that for every 10 percent differential in the import price relative to the domestic, exports to Europe are priced around 4 percent under the domestic price.

Three specific programs for supporting a two-pricing system can be identified. First, a voluntary pricing program by processors involved in exporting is desirable and, in fact, such pricing is exercised by some processors. Second, a reserve pool of concentrate owned collectively by all growers could be used as a means for providing concentrate for exports. Under this program, target prices could be set for releasing concentrate from the pool specifically for exports. This procedure represents an industry attempt to directly support a two-pricing program, while the first alternative is strictly voluntary. A third program now in existence relates to a direct subsidy to those firms involved in foreign market development. Specifically, the cost of advertising Florida citrus in foreign markets is partially paid by both the Florida Department of Citrus and the Foreign Agricultural Service of the USDA. Other programs could possibly include a direct payment subsidy to those processors actively using a two-pricing program.

Pricing Fresh Grapefruit Exports. Export trade of fresh grapefruit has become particularly important to the industry. Hence, pricing questions are of immediate importance. In general, the U.S. domestic price has been substantially below export prices, while exports to Japan have sold at a premium to all other markets. A study by Ward and Tang (1978) has shown that total industry returns could be improved by reducing the differential between Japanese and U.S. grapefruit markets. The conclusions were based on using estimated price elasticities of demand of 0.7431 for the United States and 3.5775 for Japan.

Japanese trade restrictions have been a major problem with the development of the Japan market for fresh grapefruit. Import quotas and embargoes can have a significant impact on the U.S. market, especially since the demand elasticities are so different between these markets. Using the demand models estimated by Ward and Tang, a simulated impact of Japanese trade can be shown. Using data for 1976, simulated trade restrictions indicate that the U.S. grapefruit sector would have experienced a $42 million loss in revenue. Generally, each 10 percent reduction in imports to Japan for the simulated period reduced U.S. total revenue by approximately $4.5 million. The impact from such restrictions is compounded by the reallocation of supplies from the elastic Japanese market to the inelastic domestic market. Hence, revenue losses are experienced in both markets. The simulated results further show that if all prices were equal (no price discrimination), during periods of rising supplies Japan would absorb an increasing share of the supplies, while the total consumption of the U.S., Canadian, and EEC markets would decrease. Likewise, total revenues to the sector would increase as long as Japan would absorb the increased supplies. While these results are interesting, considerable price differentials exist and, hence, actual allocations differ from those simulated.

The Japanese market for fresh grapefruit will continue to have an increasing level of importance to the long-run economic stability of the U.S. grapefruit industry. Efforts to solve those problems inhibiting trade are absolutely essential to the continued growth of the industry.

6

-
-
-
Futures Markets and Forward Pricing
-
-
-
-
-
-
-
-
-
-

The FCOJ Futures Market

Futures contracts for frozen concentrated orange juice (FCOJ) have been traded on the New York Cotton Exchange since 1967. This contract is somewhat unique among futures markets in that it has existed for several years in a market that has characteristically been oligopolistic, especially at the processing level. In the following discussion several factors are noted that should change the role of this contract as the industry evolves through time.

The FCOJ contract is defined as 15,000 pounds of orange solids ranging in grade or specification from 58 to 65 degrees brixs. Brixs are essentially a measure of pounds of solids in a gallon of juice and the sugar content. For example, there are 7.135 pounds of orange solids in one gallon of 65 degrees brixs concentrate or 378.2 pounds of solids in a 55 gallon drum. The concentrate deliverable against the contract must meet minimum scores based on empirical measures of color, flavor, and defects. For years the product was deliverable in 55 gallon drums, but since 1986 product can also be certified for delivery in bulk tanks, and in fact, this is now the predominant method in the industry. All delivery points as of this writing are located in Florida. Contract months are defined for January, March, May, July, September, and November.

Before discussing the historical performance of this market it is essential to highlight the fundamental role of futures trading in the industry. The use of FCOJ futures initially evolved out of the perceived need for the industry to have an organized mechanism for pricing inventories that must be carried throughout the crop season. Three major factors are of particular importance to the development of this contract.

First, production and harvesting schedules are such that between the months of December and July inventories must be accumulated as fruit is harvested and processed. In the latter half of the year consumption demands are primarily met through depletion of stocks. Conceptually, futures contracts are a perfect tool for allocating stocks through time, since with high forward prices stocks can be priced and carried through time. In periods of discounted future prices stocks are drawn out of storage since the forward price may not cover the full cost of storage. Second, supplies are subject to major changes due primarily to the occurrence of freezes. This produces a substantial risk in terms of processors' assurance of having adequate supplies. Finally, at the time the contract is developed no other formal forward pricing mechanism exists, thus providing the economic incentive for futures trading.

Cooperatives and individual firms provide production contracts but without any assurance of a target price. Both cooperative contracts and participation plans offered by processors essentially provide a predetermined buyer (and seller) without establishing a settling price. Producers received the average price after the oranges are processed and sold. These arrangements are typically of a wide range of "pooling programs" found throughout the U.S. agriculture system.

The orange concentrate industry has evolved in several fundamental directions in the last decade, with each having a potential effect on the role of FCOJ futures. First, consumers preferences for orange products have shifted to demand product in more convenient forms. This growth has been primarily reflected in the growth of chilled orange juice or "ready-to-serve" juice. Chilled orange juice is primarily made from the reconstitution of frozen concentrate, although during the harvest season some oranges are processed directly into the ready-to-serve containers. It is impractical to store reconstituted juice, hence the need for inventories of concentrate grew in order to provide the bulk concentrate necessary to meet the growing chilled orange juice market. This has led to a major growth in bulk storage, first in the 55 gallon drums and then in large bulk tanks often referred to as "tank farms."

The reconstitution of bulk orange concentrate into single strength ready-to-serve juices is a reasonably straightforward process in comparison to processing the initial concentrate. Reconstitution processes are such that they can be accomplished using much of the same equipment used in dairy bottling plants. Hence, the citrus industry has seen a major shifting of the reconstitution by plants outside the traditional control of the major Florida processors. This shift has added new potential traders to the market and has reduced the oligopolistic power once found among the major Florida processors. Since firms involved in the reconstitution of orange concentrate are primarily buyers of concentrate, one would expect the potential for long-term procurement through the futures market to be a viable option. Together, both the number of potential long traders should have expanded and the prevalence of price leadership lessened.

The expanding demand for bulk juice also has contributed to the growth in the imports of bulk concentrate primarily from Brazil. As noted in other chapters, imports of FCOJ have grown from under 1 million gallons in the late sixties to in excess of 100 million gallons (42 degrees brixs) in the mid-eighties. This infusion of foreign juice not only competes for the domestic industry, but also ties the forward prices more closely to the world markets for concentrate. Conceptually, the orange juice futures market should reflect these structural changes within the citrus industry.

FCOJ User Strategies. The frozen concentrated orange juice futures contract is a coordinating mechanism predominantly used by Florida processors and more recently by Brazilian traders. It has little relevance for California and Texas as a hedging mechanism. The marketing structure of the citrus industry dictates to a degree the usefulness of FCOJ futures. If an industry or a firm within an industry maintains complete control over prices, then the need for use of the futures market is questionable. Likewise, various structural arrangements such as strong vertically integrated links between producers and processors alter the types of useful hedging programs. Programs to prevent unusual supply changes such as product reserves can reduce the probability of price changes and, hence, the need for hedging.

Each trader in the industry considering hedging develops hedging plans in accordance with his or her market position within the industry. If the grower is strictly a cash fruit operator, then the grower has in no way committed fruit to be sold at a designated price. This trader is free to hedge the product. Although the fruit is uncommitted at the time of delivery, options for futures delivery are not absolute since the product is still in raw fruit form. Generally, this grower must find a home for the fruit and lift the hedge through an offsetting contract purchase (Ward and Niles 1975, 14).

The delivery options for any contract are essential to assure that the futures and cash prices remain in the proper relationship at the maturity date of the contract. As long as there is an adequate number of processors who can readily exercise the delivery options, then the cash grower would be unlikely to ever have to make delivery on a short position.

The cash grower who has forward priced fruit either through an intermediate handler or directly to a processor cannot use the futures market as a hedging tool. In essence, the grower has already fixed the price of the fruit and has no need to hedge. There is no risk of a price change to this grower.

A major share of the citrus growers commit fruit to a processor through either participation plans or cooperatives. However, the price of their product is not fixed. Such growers have the option to use the futures market to hedge their fruit, even though the grower does not have the option to deliver against the futures contract. These growers are committed to receive the average price under the pooled fruit arrangement. This average should reflect major price changes; hence, there should be a correlation between the futures price and the average price during major changes in demand or supply. The correlation between futures and the pooled fruit price should be less than between futures and the cash price. Hence, the hedging efforts of the cash trader would generally be expected to be more effective than for the trader committed to the average price. In reviewing the growers' uses of the futures, hedging pooled fruit would be less effective for the grower than hedging uncommitted fruit.

The structural arrangement of the processors will usually better facilitate the use of hedging programs. Processors forward purchase a major share of their supplies through cooperative arrangements or participation plans. These supplies are carried as inventories and can be effectively hedged. However, the motivation for hedging may differ according to the particular processor structure.

Many processors will hedge their nonpooled fruit (priced fruit) as it is carried throughout the season. The purchase price of this fruit is fixed; hence, it is the processor's equity which is subject to the price risk. In comparison, changes in the value of pooled fruit can be passed back to the grower, with the full price risk being carried by the grower. There may be less economic motivation for the processor to hedge this fruit, since the price risk can be passed on. If the processor is a cooperative, there should be an incentive for the cooperative board to protect all fruit, since ultimately all returns to the cooperative are distributed back to the grower. In contrast, the economic incentive for hedging pooled fruit by corporate processors will depend upon how the gains from hedging are shared between the processor and grower.

If a Florida processor holds concentrate in excess of normal inventory, the value of this juice could change considerably by the time it is marketed. Rather than accepting such risk, the processor could sell a near equivalent quantity of juice through the futures market, thus establishing the price of the excess inventories. A commitment is now made to deliver the designated quantity of juice at some later date. As the contract month nears, the processor may reverse the futures position through an offsetting contract purchase, or under certain circumstances the processor may wish to make delivery against the futures position. This decision will depend on the relative movement of the futures and cash market prices over the time period (Niles and Ward 1974, 290).

Traders supplying or holding a product for subsequent sale will hedge by placing short future positions. A narrowing of the basis will work to the advantage of these traders. There are clear basis patterns evident in the citrus futures which can be consistently used by the short hedgers. Citrus futures tend to be bid up relative to the cash prices in the late fall. The basis is wider at precisely the time that most short hedgers in the industry are placing their hedged position. The basis tends to narrow from a high in the October-December periods to a low in the summer. Most grower hedges would be lifted near the same time that the basis reaches a low. Therefore, both the citrus grower and processor can, with a high degree of certainty, place their hedge in the late fall and realize a basis gain when their hedges are terminated (Niles and Ward 1974, 291).

FCOJ Futures Trading Levels. Current data sources do not differentiate between types of FCOJ futures trades except to separate speculative from hedging activities for both long (buying forward) and short (selling forward) positions. For most contracts traded in the United States these positions are reported for only the large traders usually defined as those holding more than 25 contracts at one time. However, the Citrus Associates of the New York Cotton Exchange provide data on all traders, thus giving greater insight into the commercial versus speculative use of this market. Data on open interest, volume of trading, and hedging and speculative activities are reported.

Figure 6.1 provides insight into the overall trading activity in this market. Average monthly volume and open interest are shown by year. Clearly, both volume and open interest show significant variability across the years and there is no apparent trend in either trading measure. Generally, open interest is compared to the volume of trading to gain some perspective on the level of liquidity in the market. That is, are there enough turnovers in trades to assure low barriers to entering and exiting

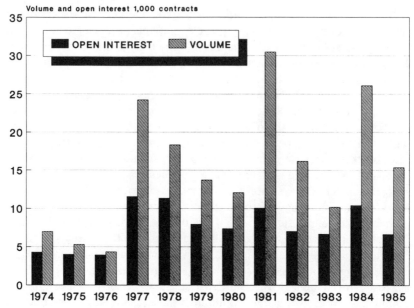

Figure 6.1. Average monthly FCOJ futures trading.

the market? As a rule the FCOJ market for most years shows a rather low volume relative to the outstanding contracts. Several studies have suggested that volume of trading needs to be at least three times the open interest to assure adequate liquidity (Behr and Ward 1984; Ward 1974). Such relative levels of trading in the FCOJ market were reflected only in 1977, 1981, and 1984. These years correspond to periods in which the industry was severely impacted by damaging freezes. Both speculative and hedging activities showed increases during these years.

Activities among the commercial and speculative traders are illustrated with Figures 6.2 through 6.6. Figures 6.2 and 6.3 show the composition of short and long positions over the year since 1974 as reflected with the monthly average for each year. The most apparent statistic gained from these two figures is the reasonably good balance of trading between hedgers and speculators. On the short side, speculation and hedging accounted for nearly 50 percent each of the total open interest. The only significant exception was in 1981 when speculative activities were predominant. The longs are illustrated in Figure 6.3 and a similar balance between hedge and speculative positions is evident. Again in 1981 the large increase in short speculative positions was primarily offset by increases in long hedges. Total commercial use of the market is illus-

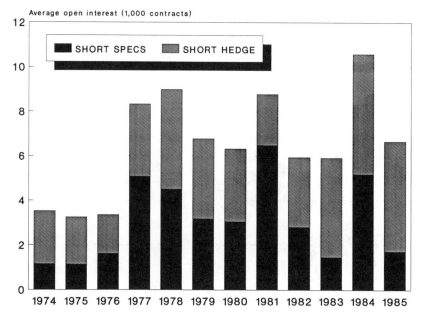

Average open interest (1,000 contracts)

Figure 6.2. Average monthly FCOJ futures short positions.

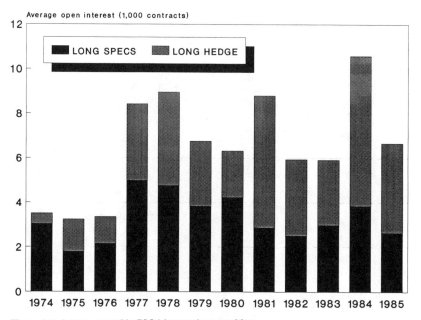

Average open interest (1,000 contracts)

Figure 6.3. Average monthly FCOJ futures long positions.

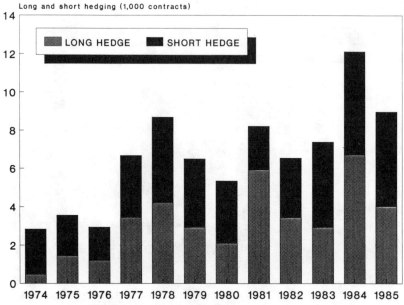

Figure 6.4. Average monthly FCOJ futures hedging positions.

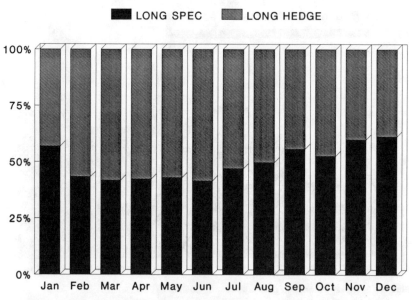

Figure 6.5. Seasonality in long FCOJ futures positions.

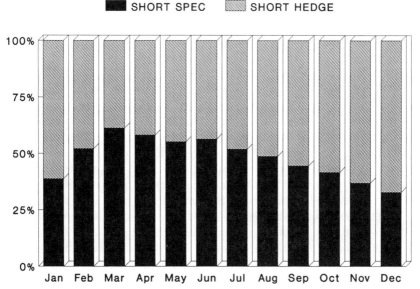

Figure 6.6. Seasonality in short FCOJ futures positions.

trated in Figure 6.4. On average the total monthly open interest has increased somewhat over the years, with the historically largest average commitments occurring in the last two years (i.e., 1984 and 1985). Likewise, commercial use by both long and short hedgers is seen throughout the years.

The predominant trend in the eighties has been a growth in both the percentage of longs and shorts held as hedged positions. Long hedges have become increasingly important. Before the eighties long hedges accounted for less than 50 percent of the total longs in terms of monthly average positions. Starting in 1981 long commercial positions showed significant increases. This commercial use of the market, starting in 1981, reflects in part the increased use of the futures market to procure concentrate following the damaging freezes in the early eighties.

Figures 6.5 and 6.6 show the seasonality in both speculative and hedged positions. Seasonality on the long side typically shows an increase in long speculative commitments, starting in September and peaking in December and January. The speculations are generally placed against the potential for price increases if a freeze occurs. In contrast, over 60 percent of the short commitments during these peak months are held by hedgers. On average then, the typical seasonal pattern is one of an increase in both long speculative and short hedged positions during the months of September through January and then a reversal of these relative positions in the other months. Note for example in Figures 6.5 and 6.6 that by March short speculations account for 60 percent of the shorts and less than 40 percent of the longs.

FCOJ Basis Patterns. Futures basis, defined as the difference between futures and spot prices, should reflect the cost of carrying stocks through time. That is, the forward price should exceed the current spot price by at least the cost of storage in order to provide the incentive to carrying stocks. When the basis falls below the storage cost, then inventories will generally be reduced simply because it is more profitable to sell in the spot market than to store the stocks. There will always, however, be some minimum level of stocks carried through time to meet planned and unplanned inventory needs. The incentive for carrying these stocks is often referred to as "convenience yield."

In addition to carrying cost and yield, the FCOJ basis has consistently shown a seasonal pattern. Starting in October the first official information about the new crop is released and this gives the first empirical benchmark for evaluating the potential for the new crop year. In the months of December, January, and February there is always the possibility of a damaging freeze destroying a share of the crop. If a freeze occurs then both spot and futures prices should increase accordingly. This potential for almost overnight losses in the crop leads to a "freeze bias" reflected in the basis starting around October. Speculators generally establish long positions, speculating on the potential for windfall gains if a freeze occurs. This "freeze bias" tends to drive the basis upward relative to normal storage costs. Following the freeze periods the freeze bias rapidly declines to zero (Malick and Ward 1987; Ward and Dasse 1977).

The general basis pattern is illustrated in Figure 6.7. The basis residual in this figure reflects the difference in the futures and cash price after removing storage and related costs. The futures price is tabulated across contract months such that the price series is always accounting for contracts that are a constant period from maturity. The CPM = 5 in Figure 6.7 denotes the constant period of maturity being set to five months and storage costs are also always for five months. The figure is reflecting a true seasonality and not changes in the contract maturity periods. The freeze bias is most apparent starting in October and peaking in December. Clearly the market is discounting the impact of a potential freeze. In this figure the basis is illustrated for three crop levels, with the level 1.0 beginning the norm. Note that the peak freeze bias is nearly identical at all three crop sizes, whereas, during the remainder of the year the levels of stocks have a major impact on the basis pattern.

The market generally becomes inverted in the summer months, that is, the market is not covering the cost of storage. Starting in these months inventories are at their peak and then will generally be drawn down during the remaining months. The inverted basis provides the incentive to drawing stocks out of storage. Note in this figure that the inversion is considerably less when stocks are above the norm. More product can be easily drawn out of storage, thus lowering the spot price and increasing the futures or forward price. The movement of product out of storage should quickly reduce an inverted market. But, when stocks are at an already low level such as reflected with the value of 0.8 in Figure 6.7, the ability for the market to fully correct the inversion is less since there may not be sufficient supplies to draw out of storage and still have adequate inventories to meet the demands for the remainder of the season. A complete detailed discussion of this basis phenomenon can be found in Malick and Ward. What is important for the current discussion, however, is to recognize the seasonal patterns to the basis.

FCOJ Trading Performance. There are four major factors a hedger can manipulate when placing a hedge: timing of the hedge, selection of the contract months, length of the hedge, and the amount hedged. Once these decisions are made, the issue of primary importance is how well the

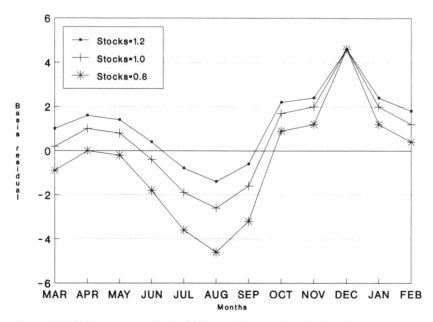

Figure 6.7. FCOJ basis seasonality for CPM = 5 and for stock level indices (.8, 1.0, 1.2).

futures contract performs. The scope of this book does not allow a detailed discussion of this issue but detailed discussions are in Tuttell (1987). One performance measure that can be readily shown, however, would be to compare the realized price from hedging to the price if a hedge were not used. At the same time the level of price risk faced with and without hedging needs to be compared. Tuttell has completed such an analysis for the FCOJ market.

Figure 6.8 shows the average spot and realized futures returns over several years. The realized price from futures trading is the calculated final selling value of the concentrate, assuming it was initially priced forward through the futures and then subsequently the futures positions were reversed. As apparent in this figure the returns from both hedged and unhedged positions followed nearly identical trends over time. On average the spot price was a few cents greater than that realized from hedging. However, the level of price risk faced with hedged positions was considerably lower than that with unhedged positions. While these results will differ by contract, months traded, and length of the hedge, the overall general conclusion is that spot returns on average will be a few cents above the realized returns using FCOJ futures but the risk level will be substantially lower with the hedged positions.

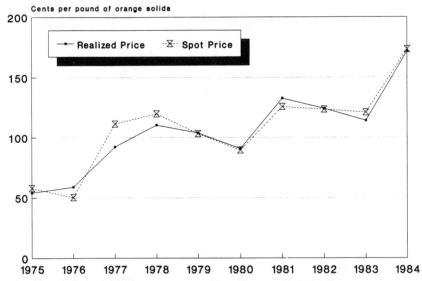

Figure 6.8. Annual realized price versus spot price for January FCOJ futures contract, 1975–84.

III

Market Development, Industry Cost, and Value

7

Citrus Advertising

•
•
•
•
•
•
•
•
•
•
•
•

The citrus industry has been a leader among those agricultural industries utilizing advertising and promotions to develop their markets. Advertising programs have been directed to both specific brands and generic orange juice products. To understand the role of advertising in the citrus industry it is essential to have some perspective regarding the ability to differentiate this product.

Two factors are of particular importance in determining the potential success of industry's promotion efforts. First, how much information about the product exists and is such information readily available? Second, can the product form be differentiated in the minds of the consumers? Generally, if a product cannot be easily differentiated but the consumers need to be reinforced to maintain consumption patterns, then the good is generally classified such that "cooperative or generic advertising" may be appropriate. That is, programs directed to establishing long-term growth and permanent consumption habits are needed. In contrast, if consumers basically know about the products but the products can be differentiated through real or fancied differences, then a strong brand program would be expected to exist. For such goods one would generally see "predatory" types of advertising leading to significant brand shifting and little total growth in demand.

Most commodities lie somewhere between these extremes, thus pointing to the potential use of both generic and brand advertising efforts. Processed citrus falls within these ranges. First, all orange juice has certain desirable characteristics such as flavor, color, health benefits, and storability common to all brands. Established as well as new orange juice consumers must be continually stimulated with this information to encourage repeat consumption. Yet the same product can be differentiated through packaging, juice sources, quality standards, and container sizes. Given these characteristics, one would expect to see both generic and brand advertising programs coexist.

Supporting Advertising Structure

Brand advertising is directed toward the purchase of specific brands of orange juice, whereas generic efforts are directed to the total product category. The funding sources for brand advertising are usually from the private firms and their parent companies. However, there have been occasions where brand advertising has been partially supported through joint ventures with the generic programs. In contrast, Florida's generic citrus advertising programs are funded primarily through the Florida Department of Citrus. Other citrus-producing states have generic programs but are generally on a small scale relative to Florida's generic advertising efforts. The Department of Citrus, operating under a state market order, taxes all commercially produced Florida citrus and other citrus juices entering the state. These funds are used to support the generic advertising programs along with quality control, market development, and marketing policy activities. The generic programs, while promoting the consumption of both fresh and processed citrus, are tied to Florida through various forms of product labeling.

In recent years part of Florida's generic advertising funds have been used to underwrite a portion of brand advertising programs through an advertising rebate program. That is, brand advertisers of citrus meeting certain predetermined advertising criteria can receive a rebate from the generic pool of funds. This program is referred to as the BAR, or brand advertising rebate program.

Given the homogeneous nature of citrus juices, the advertising programs generally lead to an expansion in demand for all citrus juices regardless of juice sources including the increasing sales of imported juices. (See Chapter 9 for a discussion of import issues.) As more imported orange concentrate enters the U.S. markets through ports outside of Florida, the issue of supporting national generic advertising efforts by Florida producers will be of even greater concern.

Several major agricultural industries in the United States have turned to national advertising programs through federally approved advertising and research acts (U.S. Department of Agriculture). These acts provide a mechanism whereby all parties supplying product in the market are subject to paying their pro rata share of the cost of generic advertising. These taxes also apply to imported product. The citrus industry currently does not have a national basis for taxing imports and other sources to jointly support national and international advertising of citrus products.

Generic and Brand Expenditures

Figure 7.1 shows the actual and relative expenditures for both brand and generic advertising of orange juice. These data are reported bimonthly for both radio and television. Since late 1983 the Florida Department of Citrus has maintained a joint venture advertising program with private processors. Hence, the brand expenditures in this figure include the advertising rebate credits received by these processors. Similarly, the generic funds do not reflect the generic allocations to the brand programs. Figure 7.1 illustrates the bimonthly variability in citrus advertising, while Figure 7.2 better illustrates the longer term growth during the eighties.

From 1979 through 1987 total citrus advertising increased from under $30 million annually to over $60 million. Most of the growth in

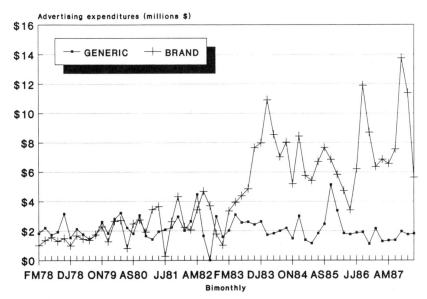

Figure 7.1. Bimonthly advertising expenditures for all orange juice. *(From Nielsen Marketing Service)*

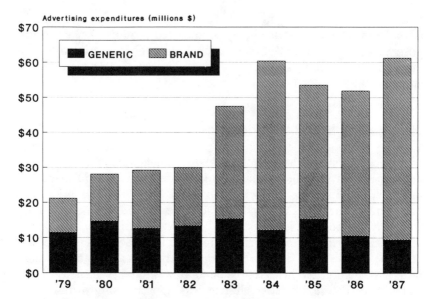

Figure 7.2. Annual advertising expenditures on all citrus juices. *(From Nielsen Marketing Service)*

citrus advertising in the eighties has been due to brand programs. In 1986 and 1987 brand programs represented over 75 percent of the total citrus advertising. A substantial share in the increased growth since 1985 is due to increased advertising activity by one major processor. Likewise, the majority of the brand programs are conducted by three major Florida processors.

Citrus Advertising Effectiveness

Several studies have been completed over the years attempting to measure the effects of citrus advertising efforts. While results differ by time periods used, data sources, and the general nature of the models, there are several common elements found among all of the studies. First, the effects of citrus advertising can be measured and every study points to a lagged effect or long-term carryover from advertising citrus. Most studies have used some form of a distributed lag structure to capture these carryover effects. Second, advertising has been measured according to expenditure levels generally expressing the levels on a real per capita basis.

The results in Table 7.1 show a revised estimate of the overall effects of generic and brand citrus advertising using the data shown in Figure 7.1 (Ward 1988). Sales are expressed in single strength equivalent gallons of orange juice including both chilled orange juices and frozen concentrate in retail packs. Likewise, the price (DPR) is a real weighted average price for both juice forms. Income (LINC) is also expressed in real per capita terms. The model is estimated using separate distributed lag specifications for generic and brand advertising with both types of advertising being expressed in log form. The coefficients for LG and LB in Table 7.1 reflect the advertising effects using polynomial lags with end point restrictions (Ward 1988).

The analyses show both generic and brand advertising to have a positive impact on total orange juice consumption. Furthermore, the generic and brand effects differ in both their immediate and long-term

Table 7.1. Estimated demand for all orange juice using a distributed lag advertising model.

DEPENDENT VARIABLE:	PER CAPITA ORANGE JUICE CONSUMPTION	
VARIABLE	ESTIMATED COEFFICIENT	T-STATISTIC
CONSTANT	-2.02270	-1.9226
PRICE	-0.46894	-12.568
PRICE ADJ	-0.07884	-6.2932
INCOME	+0.41595	+3.2719
D2	+0.00669	+0.8206
D4	-0.01500	-1.9677
D6	-0.04486	-5.6275
D8	-0.03436	-4.3819
D10	-0.01785	-2.7201
LG1	+0.00340	+2.4789
LG2	+0.00393	+2.0447
LB1	+0.00774	+2.5756

	GENERIC			BRAND	
LAG	COEFF	T-STAT	LAG	COEFF	T-STAT
0	0.0034	2.4789	0	0.0077	2.5756
1	0.0040	3.2470	1	0.0066	2.5756
2	0.0042	2.7816	2	0.0055	2.5756
3	0.0042	2.3304	3	0.0044	2.5756
4	0.0039	2.0447	4	0.0033	2.5756
5	0.0034	1.8593	5	0.0022	2.5756
6	0.0025	1.7318	6	0.0011	2.5756
7	0.0014	1.6395			
SUM	0.0270			0.0310	

SUM OF SQUARED RESIDUALS	=0.010300
STANDARD ERROR OF THE REGRESSION	=0.016046
MEAN OF DEPENDENT VARIABLE	=0.578350
STANDARD DEVIATION	=0.036940
R-SQUARED	=0.852000
ADJUSTED R-SQUARED	=0.811300
DURBIN-WATSON STATISTIC	=1.3378
F-STATISTIC(11,40)	=20.9337
LOG OF LIKELIHOOD FUNCTION	=147.913
NUMBER OF OBSERVATIONS	=52

responses. Figure 7.3 illustrates the current and long-term effects of generic and brand advertising. The solid bars measure the immediate impact of generic advertising on orange juice consumption over current and lagged period. Comparing the bars across lagged advertising periods shows the peak effect occuring in the third bimonthly period and then the remaining generic advertising effects declining for the next several bimonthly periods. There is a significant immediate effect to generic advertising and a significant long-term or cumulative effect. This pattern to generic citrus advertising effectiveness is similar to what has been shown for the fluid milk market and what has been measured from earlier studies of the orange juice advertising programs (Ward and Myers 1979).

Figure 7.3 also includes the brand advertising parameters for the same periods measured for the generic. Brand advertising has its greatest impact on orange juice consumption in the current period and also has a long-term effect similar to that for generic. Subsequent brand advertising effects decline for all remaining periods after the first. The results are totally consistent with the advertising literature. Brand advertising has its greatest impact in the current period with a continued decline measured for later periods. Generic advertising has a lower immediate impact and a slightly larger impact after several months. Both show

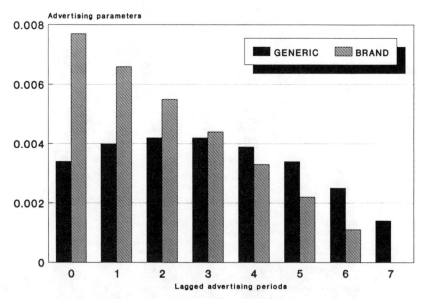

Figure 7.3. Generic and brand advertising responses for all orange juice.

significant long-term effects on total orange juice consumption. The empirical results clearly indicate that brand advertising has supported total orange juice consumption and that generic and brand advertising have different impacts on consumer purchasing behavior.

The model can be used to estimate the gains in all orange juice sales attributed to generic and brand advertising. Given actual generic and brand advertising data, the econometric model was used to predict total orange juice sales. Then using the same model, sales were predicted assuming a minimal level of advertising. The difference between the first and second values represents the sales gains attributed to all advertising. Finally, sales were predicted using actual generic expenditures while holding brand levels to a minimum. The difference represents the gains due to brand advertising. Predicted sales for all advertising and minimal advertising are illustrated in Figure 7.4. The differences represent the gains resulting from all advertising and then that attributed to generic and brand separately. The relative contributions of both generic and brand are clear in this figure.

Over the period from 1984 through 1987 all generic advertising is calculated to have contributed to a 7.95 percent increase in consumption above that predicted with an assumed minimal level of advertising. In comparison, brand advertising generated a 17.5 percent increase in all

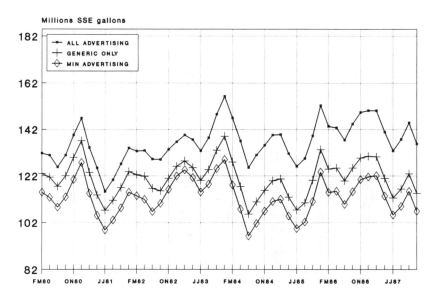

Figure 7.4. Estimated orange juice sales with minimal advertising, generic advertising, and brand advertising.

orange juice sales for the same periods. While these percentages will differ given the expenditures levels, the major thing to see from the analysis is that both types of advertising have been instrumental in supporting the consumption of orange juice.

The analysis indicated that generic advertising has generated approximately 45 to 50 million single strength gallon increases annually over what would have occurred with the minimal assumed advertising level (see Figure 7.5). During the early eighties gains attributed to brand were roughly the same as generic. After 1983 annual gains resulting from expanded brand advertising led to annual increases in excess of 100 million single strength gallons. In 1987 the brand effect equaled 124.7 million single strength gallons. By 1987 gains from brand advertising represented nearly 75 percent of the total predicted gains over minimal advertising levels.

Retail revenue gains from both generic and brand can be compared. For periods since 1983 brand advertising generated revenue gains of around 18 percent above that with only minimal advertising while the gains associated with generic advertising were nearly 8 percent above the predicted base sales using only a minimal level of generic and brand advertising.

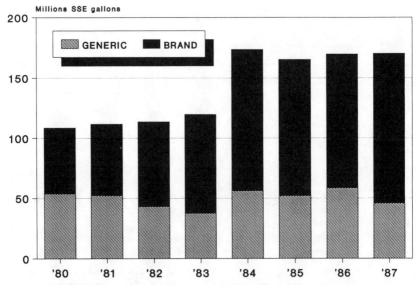

Figure 7.5. Gains in orange juice sales due to generic and brand advertising.

Selected Generic Programs

The citrus industry has been innovative in trying several forms of generic advertising plans. Retail incentive programs where retail chains advertise with the Florida Department of Citrus sharing in the costs have been supported on occasion. Joint ventures between processors and generic efforts have been utilized in the last several seasons to some extent. The Department of Citrus has used plans whereby private label products can carry the Florida citrus seal of quality, thus assuring the consumer of the product standards. Coupon programs have been used extensively over the years. Studies by Ward and Davis (1978b) and more recent revisions by Lee and Brown (1985) clearly show coupons to be effective in enhancing the demand for citrus juices. These models not only show the effects of coupons on sales, but also can be used to address issues of how best to distribute citrus coupons. Ward and Davis (1978a) showed the greatest redemption rates to occur with direct mailing and the lowest with on-package redemption. Similarly they measured the redemption rates according to the face value of the coupons. While considerably greater detail can be found in these studies, they all point to the positive marginal gains from the citrus efforts.

The Florida citrus industry has participated in efforts to expand international markets through direct personnel involvement in the foreign markets and through international advertising efforts. Joint ventures among the Florida industry, the Foreign Agricultural Service (FAS), and the foreign importer have been utilized for several years. A three-party program where these three parties share in the advertising activities has been the primary instrument for generic promotions in the international marketplace. A study by Lee (1977) shows strong consumption responses to these activities. The generic contributions to the three-party programs have ranged up to approximately $800,000. There has been considerable variability in the annual contributions, and in recent years Florida contributions have dropped to around $250,000. Part of this decline is attributed to the reduced crop sizes due to several freezes.

Finally, as noted in the chapters dealing with trade, imports accounted for an increasing share of the U.S. market. An increasing share of these imported juices is not subject to advertising taxes since it is imported into ports outside of Florida. Most of these juices originate in Brazil. Brazil does not actively participate in the advertising and promotion of their product in the U.S. markets. It provides a juice source that must be reprocessed and hence has little direct incentive to establish brands or promote domestic consumption. This situation may change as Florida recovers from significant crop losses of the early eighties.

8

Industry Cost
and Value

Technology and Cost

While the previous sections identified the structure which facilitates movement of citrus through the vertical marketing system, it is of equal importance to have an understanding of the state of technology and the associated cost of distributing processed and fresh citrus. Four costs are of particular importance to the industry: (1) production cost, (2) picking and hauling, (3) packing and/or processing, and (4) selling. Changes in these costs reflect not only the expected inflation impact on the industry but also show the degree of capital intensity and state of technology.

The cost of production, picking and hauling, processing packing, and selling appear in annual reports which have been published for the past 30 years by the Food and Resource Economics Department, University of Florida. The studies are based on the accounting data of firms that are willing to participate. The California data are based on the *Citrus Fruit Industry Statistical Bulletin,* Sunkist Growers, Inc.

Production Cost. Production costs on a per box basis have been increasing in Florida but at a rate less than in California (Figure 8.1). From 1976–77 through 1986–87 the estimated annual per acre costs and returns for a mature, round orange grove in Florida increased 91.8 percent (Table 8.1). The management fee increased the most (229.4 percent) followed by weed control (198.2 percent), pruning (128.9 percent), and

108

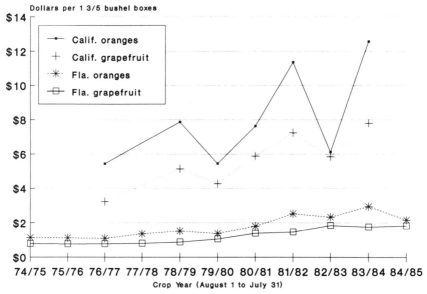

Figure 8.1. Grove cost for producing oranges and grapefruit in Florida and California. *(From Florida Crop and Livestock Reporting Service and Sunkist Growers)*

Table 8.1 Estimated annual per acre costs and returns for a mature, round orange grove producing citrus for processing in Florida, 1976-77 through 1986-87.

em	1976-77	1977-78	1978-79	1979-80	1980-81	Season[a] 1981-82	1982-83	1983-84	1984-85	1985-86	1986-87
eed control	31.25	33.03	37.12	42.09	46.44	49.57	51.16	100.00	103.69	91.93	93.18
·ray program	76.73	78.14	84.81	111.95	129.98	135.53	143.57	142.10	147.33	148.66	155.81
rtilizer	49.25	48.55	50.12	57.27	89.52	99.89	96.87	100.41	97.30	91.27	96.41
olomite	5.09	4.80	6.25	5.66	9.61	8.36	10.16	8.36	10.97	9.85	9.09
·uning (maintenance)	13.28	21.94	23.31	26.08	23.92	23.05	24.95	25.49	28.86	29.10	30.40
·ee replacement and care	39.49	40.82	47.23	54.74	58.51	62.47	62.29	54.18	59.89	52.57	53.77
·rigation (operating cost)	99.46	101.05	103.88	137.42	103.18	108.12	111.93	115.39	120.57	117.33	121.09
anagement	31.64	65.77	82.42	59.11	78.33	81.23	104.64	100.94	128.23	77.37	104.23
OTAL	346.19	394.10	435.14	494.32	539.49	568.22	605.57	646.87	696.8	618.08	663.98

·urce: Muraro.
august 1 through July 31.

spray program (103.1 percent). The spray program made up the largest percentage of total costs (23.5 percent) in 1986–87, followed by the irrigation cost (18.2 percent), management (15.7 percent), fertilizer (14.5 percent), and weed control (14 percent). When yield starts to level off in Florida, a per box cost increase similar to that in California is likely to evolve unless input costs are reduced.

Picking and Hauling. Picking and hauling costs have trended upward in both California and Florida, with Florida having lower costs (Figure 8.2 and Table 8.2). From 1960–61 through 1982–83 picking labor costs per box increased 223 percentage points; other labor increased 241 percentage points; and fuel, oil, repairs, and depreciation increased 195 percentage points. All labor represented 72.1 percent of total costs in 1982–83 which indicates the labor-intensive nature of picking and hauling.

Processing Cost. The cost of processing in Florida has trended upward since 1965–66 (Figures 8.3 and 8.4). Materials were the largest cost item at 40.4 percent of total costs in 1982–83, followed by other process-

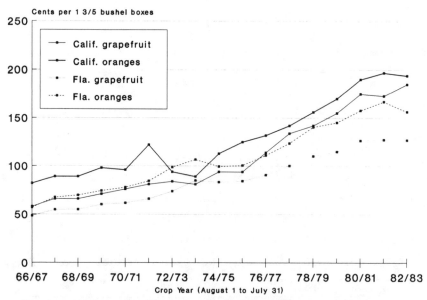

Figure 8.2. Picking and hauling cost for oranges and grapefruit in Florida and California. *(From Hooks and Sunkist Growers)*

Table 8.2. Changes in the cost items that make up estimated total picking and hauling costs for Florida oranges, 1960-61 through 1982-83.

Season[a]	Picking labor		Other labor[b]		Fuel, oil repairs, depreciation		Administrative and other[c]	
	¢/box	Index[d]	¢/box	Index[d]	¢/box	Index[d]	¢/box	Index[d]
1960-61	18.90	85	12.52	96	8.37	91	6.34	100
1961-62	19.64	88	12.17	93	7.56	82	4.83	76
1962-63	22.50	101	13.29	101	9.98	109	6.74	107
1963-64	24.24	109	14.17	108	10.33	112	8.03	127
1964-65	26.38	118	13.35	102	9.72	106	5.64	89
1965-66	28.54	128	14.43	110	9.88	107	5.23	83
1966-67	29.53	132	13.79	105	8.42	92	5.25	83
1967-68	33.42	150	16.96	129	10.88	118	6.15	97
1968-69	37.51	168	15.69	120	10.82	118	5.73	91
1969-70	38.54	173	17.00	130	12.32	134	6.44	102
1970-71	38.70	173	17.99	137	12.75	139	8.46	134
1971-72	40.91	183	22.34	171	13.38	145	7.83	124
1972-73	52.60	236	22.00	168	15.06	164	7.20	114
1973-74	57.86	259	23.10	176	16.57	180	9.21	146
1974-75	51.87	232	22.87	175	16.53	180	8.25	131
1975-76	50.61	227	25.52	195	17.38	189	7.20	114
1976-77	54.96	246	27.60	211	19.29	210	9.34	148
1977-78	58.96	264	33.46	255	20.34	221	10.92	173
1978-79	65.76	294	40.31	308	23.32	254	11.08	175
1979-80	67.82	304	39.60	302	25.47	277	12.32	195
1980-81	72.92	327	44.37	339	26.83	292	13.80	218
1981-82	73.64	330	46.56	355	28.43	309	18.40	291
1982-83	68.72	308	44.14	337	26.31	286	17.43	276

Source: Hooks, various issues (b).
[a]August 1 through July 31.
[b]Includes supervisory, loaders, drivers, semi-drivers, miscellaneous and payroll taxes, and workmen's compensation.
[c]Includes licenses, taxes, insurance, supplies, equipment rental, migratory labor expense, and miscellaneous costs.
[d]The index is the yearly cost as a percent of the 1960-61 to 1964-65 average cost.

ing costs at 19.5 percent (Table 8.3). Labor represented only 12.3 percent. A few processors own their own can manufacturing plants and realized considerable savings on cans. Selling costs equaled 6.7 percent. Because of the seasonal nature of citrus grove production, warehousing represented 6.9 percent of total costs. Total processing costs for orange concentrate increased 113 percent over the base period of 1965–68. Materials, the largest component of total cost, increased 91 percent. Other processing costs, which include power, water, lights, steam, maintenance, repairs, royalties, taxes, insurance, and rent, increased 170 percent over the base period of 1965–68.

Packing and Selling Costs. Packing and selling costs for Florida and California citrus have trended up since 1966–67, as shown in Figures 8.3 and 8.4. In 1981–82 materials were 27.1 percent of total packing and

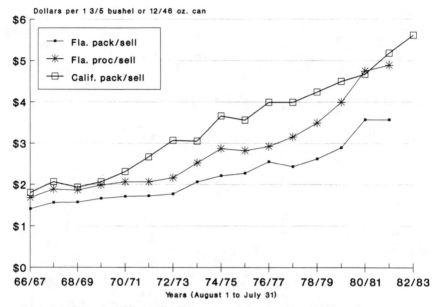

Figure 8.3. Cost of packing and selling, processing and selling Florida and California grapefruit. *(From Hooks and Sunkist Growers)*

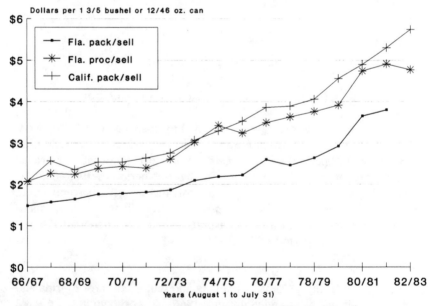

Figure 8.4. Cost of packing and selling, processing and selling Florida and California oranges. *(From Hooks and Sunkist Growers)*

112

Table 8.3. The relative changes in the component costs that make up the total cost of processing, warehousing, and selling 48 6 ounce Florida orange concentrate, 1965-66 through 1982-83.

Season	Materials		Labor		Other Processing[a]		Warehousing		Administrative		Selling		Other		Total	
	$/case	Index	$/case	Index	$/case	Index	$/case	Index	$/case	Index	$/case	Index	$/case	Index	$/case	Index
1965-66	0.9982	99	0.2656	106	0.3872	112	0.1234	100	0.1444	128	0.1519	123	0.3163	116	2.3870	107
1966-67	1.0208	101	0.2117	85	0.2759	80	0.1053	86	0.0766	68	0.0935	76	0.2825	104	2.0663	92
1967-68	1.0128	100	0.2729	109	0.3705	108	0.1395	114	0.1180	104	0.1249	101	0.2164	80	2.2550	101
1968-69	1.0279	102	0.2776	111	0.3380	98	0.1112	91	0.1203	106	0.1169	95	0.2481	91	2.2400	100
1969-70	1.0271	102	0.2943	118	0.3355	97	0.1278	104	0.1211	107	0.1223	99	0.3556	131	2.3837	107
1970-71	1.0627	105	0.2881	115	0.3789	109	0.1354	110	0.1390	123	0.1514	127	0.2737	101	2.4272	109
1971-72	1.0771	107	0.2666	108	0.3728	108	0.1147	93	0.1623	143	0.1270	103	0.2646	97	2.3851	107
1972-73	1.1815	117	0.2978	119	0.4170	121	0.1358	111	0.1761	156	0.1389	113	0.2639	97	2.6110	117
1973-74	1.3285	131	0.3865	155	0.4864	141	0.1930	157	0.1521	135	0.1279	104	0.3483	122	3.0227	135
1974-75	1.6534	164	0.3654	146	0.5130	149	0.2240	182	0.1636	145	0.1566	127	0.3435	126	3.4194	153
1975-76	1.5213	151	0.3394	136	0.5468	159	0.2005	163	0.1247	110	0.1490	121	0.3622	133	3.2439	145
1976-77	1.4557	144	0.4463	178	0.6302	183	0.2196	179	0.1460	129	0.2006	163	0.3900	144	3.4884	156
1977-78	1.5049	149	0.4517	181	0.6854	199	0.2204	179	0.1323	117	0.2239	181	0.4099	151	3.6285	162
1978-79	1.6011	158	0.4515	181	0.6615	192	0.2268	185	0.1563	138	0.2063	167	0.4562	168	3.7597	168
1979-80	1.7419	172	0.4779	191	0.6954	202	0.2310	188	0.1512	134	0.2244	182	0.3848	142	3.9066	175
1980-81[b]	1.8718	185	0.6035	241	0.9106	264	0.2998	244	0.2269	201	0.2725	221	0.5558	205	4.7409	212
1981-82[c]	1.9246	190	0.6225	249	0.9407	273	0.3227	263	0.2009	178	0.3216	261	0.5796	213	4.9126	220
1982-83[c]	1.9252	191	0.5879	235	0.9316	270	0.3283	267	0.1923	170	0.3195	259	0.4814	177	4.7662	213
Base[d]	1.0106	100	0.2501	100	0.3445	100	0.1228	100	0.1130	100	0.1234	100	0.2717	100	2.2361	100

Source: Hooks, various issues (c).
[a] Includes power, water, lights, steam, maintenance, repairs, royalties, taxes, insurance, rent, and miscellaneous.
[b] 1980-81 brix is 43.4; prior years are 45 brix.
[c] Brix is 42.
[d] The index for each item was computed as a percentage of the 1965-68 average cost (shown in the last row of the table).

selling costs; labor was 30.5 percent; power, maintenance, and supplies were 8.8 percent; insurance, taxes, and depreciation were 6.7 percent; administrative expense was 7.2 percent; selling was 6.5 percent; and miscellaneous expense was 13.2 percent for packing and selling oranges in 1⅗ bushel boxes in Florida (Table 8.4).

Capacity is an important factor influencing average packing cost. The cost differential between a small plant (100,000–500,000 1⅗ bushel boxes) and the most efficient size plant (500,000–850,000 1⅗ bushel boxes) is 41 cents per box or 14 percent of costs of a large plant. Therefore, some of the small plants are operating at a size disadvantage. In the short run, managers of plants of less than optimal size can manipulate

Table 8.4. Weighted average costs of packing and selling Florida oranges per 1 3/5 bushel equivalent, 1981-82 season.

Item of cost	Dollars per 1 3/5 bushel equivalent
Materials	
Containers	0.9889
Other materials	0.0410
Total materials	1.0299
Labor	
Receive, truck, dump	0.0887
Crate making and labeling	0.1112
Foremen, graders, others	0.3737
Packing	0.2388
Truck, check, load	0.1812
Payroll taxes, comp. ins.	0.1662
Total labor	1.1598
Other direct operating	
Power, lights, water	0.0945
Repairs and maintenance	0.1630
Misc. supplies and expenses	0.0752
Total other direct	0.3327
Indirect operating	
Insurance-fire and casuality	0.0288
Taxes and licenses	0.0451
Depreciation and rent	0.1790
Total indirect operating	0.2529
Total packing expense	2.7753
Administrative	0.2726
Selling	0.2464
Other items	0.5028
Total cost	3.7971

Source: Hooks, various issues (a).

capacity utilization, packout percentage, season length, and supply variability in order to reduce costs.

Capacity utilization by packinghouses packing more than 100,000 1⅗ bushel boxes varied from 19 to 90 percent between 1975 and 1976 with an average of 50 percent. This was based on an 11-month operating season. The cost differential between these two extremes is 62 cents or 27 percent of a firm with a capacity utilization of 90 percent (Kilmer and Tilley 1978, 8). The average packinghouse utilization is highly variable. This is due to the variability in the number of packinghouses shipping fruit in a given year and the total quantity to be packed.

Between the 1964–65 and 1965–66 seasons packinghouses actually packing fruit increased by 65 houses. The average volume packed has been as low as 118,340 1⅗ bushel boxes in the 1962–63 season and 242,771 in the 1978–79 season. Between the 1975–76 and 1976–77 seasons average volume packed dropped by 55,089 boxes because of freeze damage to the crop, which rendered the fruit quality unacceptable for fresh use. Aided by a labor intensive technology and depreciated capital assets, packinghouses remain idle in those years when crop size is down and/or the price is not favorable for packing fruit.

Packout percentage among the packinghouses ranges from 30 percent to 88 percent. The cost differential between these two extremes is 28 cents or 11.4 percent of a firm with a packout percentage of 88 (Kilmer and Tilley 1978, 8). Given that many packinghouses are cooperatives with grove caretaking operations, production practices that result in high packout fruit can be used to help reduce packing cost.

Finally, the season length ranged from 19 to 46 weeks, and weekly supply variability measured by the inverse of the coefficient of variation ranged from 0.23 to 1.43. Each variable resulted in a cost differential of three cents between extremes (Kilmer and Tilley 1978, 8). The relatively high standard errors of the coefficients indicate that firms were able to make resource adjustments so that length and variability of supply did not materially affect costs. This reflects the fact that most workers in a packinghouse work on a piece rate or hourly basis and are not paid when fruit is unavailable.

The operating characteristics, pack variability, and proportion of oranges to grapefruit packed are dependent on the type of package desired by wholesale buyers as well as availability and quality of fruit in the area served by the packinghouse. Pack variability among firms ranges from 0 to 83 percent. That is, some firms pack all of their product in standard cartons, while others pack as much as 83 percent in nonstandard packages. The cost differential between the two extremes is 25 cents or 10 percent of the average cost of a plant with all packs being standard cartons (Kilmer and Tilley 1978, 9). This is nearly as important as pack-out percentage, but the manager must pack different types of packages to meet buyers' orders. Managers may be able to make more profit because of increased revenues from nonstandard packages regardless of the extra cost of packing different package types.

Packinghouses with a high proportion of oranges were found to have lower costs than houses packing a high proportion of grapefruit. This may reflect the fact that grapefruit are shipped in heavier, more expensive cartons. The cost differential between the minimum and maximum values was 36 cents or 15 percent of the packing costs for an average firm at $2.44.

In summary, capacity utilization and packout percentage will increase competition among Florida citrus packinghouses in the short run. In the longer term, average plant capacity will increase as the advantage of lower cost at higher capacity makes it increasingly difficult for small plants to remain cost competitive. Large plants can realize the same cost savings available through increased capacity utilization and packout percentage as small plants.

Significant potential for improved industry cost performance exists in the packinghouse industry. A capacity utilization of 50 percent and a packout percentage of 63 percent are an indication of the high potential currently existing for improvement in industry technical efficiency. The industry is not only underutilizing capacity, but also many plants are operating at nonoptimal sizes.

The improvement in technical efficiency will be slow; however, underutilization of capacity is present for several reasons. First, the packinghouses with less mechanized technology have a 16 cent lower packing cost than more mechanized houses. If labor remains available at reasonable cost the older houses will continue to operate for several years. Second, improved coordination is needed between the grower and packer in order to increase the packing season length. Currently citrus is packed on the average of 36 weeks in each house, with a minimum of 19 and a maximum of 46 weeks. An increase in volume packed is assumed when the packing season is lengthened. In order for this to occur fresh fruit shipments must increase and/or the number of houses packing fruit must decrease. Finally, extension personnel and members of boards of directors may need to reevaluate management that is just as cost efficient as a large packinghouse.

The southerly shift in citrus production will have a small effect on existing packinghouse size and location over the next decade unless the trees killed by freezing are not replanted in the north. In this case packinghouses will be closed permanently.

Costs of Marketing Channel Functions. In order to complete the marketing channel, transportation, wholesaling, and retailing costs in addition to f.o.b., shipping point and retail prices need to be available. Unfortunately, few of the data needed to examine the components of the f.o.b. retail margin are available for specific products. However, the f.o.b. retail price differential can be examined to determine the nature of changes in the relationship for several seasons for fresh grapefruit, frozen concentrated orange juice, and canned single strength grapefruit juice. Even then, data on f.o.b. prices are not perfect because sales at prices that deviate from card or posted prices are generally not publicized or reported. In addition, f.o.b. prices for advertised branded products were not available.

It must be emphasized that only relative changes in the marketing margin can be measured and that little can be said about wholesale or retail profit levels. In addition, because of the nature of a retail outlet, it is possible that a retailer may have very low or negative margins on certain products in order to generate traffic through the store and sell products with higher unit profits. The extent to which citrus and citrus products are used as loss leaders is not known.

The f.o.b. retail margin accounts for over 60 percent of the retail value of fresh fruit (Table 8.5). Less than 40 percent of the retail price paid for fresh Florida grapefruit is paid for growing, picking and hauling, and packing and selling. On the other hand, the f.o.b. retail margins for frozen concentrated orange juice and canned single strength grapefruit juice average 25 and 27 percent of retail value (Tables 8.6 and 8.7). No trend in the f.o.b. retail margin is evident except for FCOJ where the trend is downward (Table 8.6).

While previous sections have been concerned with stages in the marketing channel, the purpose of this section is to simultaneously look at the total marketing channel and determine how much of the consumer's dollar spent on citrus and citrus products is returned to various marketing channel participants. Three products, orange concentrate, canned single strength grapefruit juice, and fresh grapefruit, are examined.

The amount and percentage of the retail dollar that is returned at various levels in the marketing channel are calculated for frozen concentrated orange juice (Table 8.6). The processing cost share has the lowest coefficient of variation (12.21 percent). The coefficient of variation for the f.o.b. retail margin share, the picking and hauling cost share, and on-tree value plus marketing firm profits share is 15.62, 17.29, and 18.01 percent, indicating an increase in variability.

For the 19 years shown, on-tree returns averaged 35 percent of the

Table 8.5. Proportion of the consumer's retail food dollar spent on fresh grapefruit that is returned to various marketing channel participants, 1964-65 through 1983-84 seasons.

Season	Retail value[ab]	Retail share[ab]	F.o.b.-retail margin[c]	F.o.b.-retail margin share[c]	Packing cost[de]	Packing cost share	Picking and hauling cost[de]	Picking and hauling cost share	On-tree value + marketing firm profit[fg]	On-tree value + mkt. firm profits share
	$/box	Percent	$/box	Percent	$/box	Percent	$/box	Percent	$/box	Percent
1964-65	10.57	100	6.53	62	1.37	13	0.45	4	2.22	21
1965-66	10.00	100	5.77	58	1.41	14	0.50	5	2.32	23
1966-67	9.33	100	5.96	64	1.41	15	0.48	5	1.48	16
1967-68	10.85	100	5.85	54	1.56	14	0.55	5	2.89	27
1968-69	11.03	100	7.18	65	1.57	14	0.55	5	1.73	16
1969-70	11.48	100	7.05	61	1.66	14	0.60	5	2.17	19
1970-71	11.22	100	6.66	59	1.71	15	0.62	6	2.23	20
1971-72	12.54	100	7.23	58	1.72	14	0.66	5	2.93	23
1972-73	13.47	100	7.99	59	1.77	13	0.74	6	2.97	22
1973-74	13.97	100	8.85	63	2.06	15	0.85	6	2.21	16
1974-75	15.02	100	9.41	63	2.21	15	0.83	6	2.57	17
1975-76	14.48	100	9.22	64	2.27	16	0.85	6	2.14	15
1976-77	15.76	100	10.14	64	2.55	16	0.91	6	2.16	14
1977-78	16.58[h]	100	11.12	67	2.43	15	0.82	5	2.21	13
1978-79	19.50[h]	100	12.56	64	2.62	13	0.90	5	3.42	18
1979-80	19.91[h]	100	11.86	60	2.89	15	1.15	6	4.01	20
1980-81	22.18[h]	100	13.17	59	3.57	16	1.27	6	4.17	19
1981-82	24.00[h]	100	15.97	67	3.57	15	1.28	5	3.18	13
1982-83	24.96[h]	100	16.92	69	--	--	1.27	5	--	--
1983-84	24.60[h]	100	16.46	67	--	--	--	--	--	--

[a]Unpublished USDA data.
[b]Six-month weighted average (November-April). White seedless, size 40, packed in two 4/5 bushel cartons, average for Atlanta, Boston, Chicago, and Pittsburgh.
[c]Calculated using the Growers Administrative Committee and Florida Citrus Mutual.
[d]Costs do not include profits.
[e]Hooks, various issues (b); Hooks and Kilmer, various issues (a).
[f]This value includes pick and haul and packinghouse firm profits.
[g]Calculated: On-tree equals retail value minus f.o.b.-retail margin minus packing cost minus picking and hauling cost.
[h]Six-month weighted average (November-April), white seedless, in two 4/5 bushel cartons, average for Baltimore and Boston.

Table 8.6   Proportion of the consumer's retail food dollar spent on 6 ounce cans of frozen concentrated orange juice that is returned to various marketing channel participants, 1964-65 through 1983-84 seasons.

Season	Retail value[a]	Retail share	F.o.b.-retail margin[b]	F.o.b.-retail margin share	Processing cost[cd]	Processing cost share	Picking and hauling cost[ce]	Picking and hauling cost share	On-tree value + marketing firm profit[fg]	On-tree value + mkt. firm profits share
	$/doz.	Percent	$/doz.	Percent	$/doz.	Percent	$/doz.	Percent	$/doz.	Percent
1964-65	2.32	100	0.70	30	0.54	23	0.19	8	0.89	38
1965-66	2.20	100	0.58	26	0.59	27	0.26	12	0.77	35
1966-67	1.75	100	0.56	32	0.52	30	0.24	14	0.43	25
1967-68	2.11	100	0.48	23	0.56	27	0.28	13	0.79	37
1968-69	2.41	100	0.63	26	0.56	23	0.35	15	0.87	36
1969-70	2.21	100	0.74	33	0.60	27	0.34	15	0.53	24
1970-71	2.23	100	0.63	28	0.61	27	0.36	16	0.63	28
1971-72	2.46	100	0.58	24	0.60	24	0.37	15	0.91	37
1972-73	2.39	100	0.66	28	0.67	28	0.41	17	0.65	27
1973-74	2.44	100	0.61	25	0.76	31	0.46	19	0.61	25
1974-75	2.61	100	0.58	22	0.60	23	0.43	16	1.00	38
1975-76	2.64	100	0.61	23	0.81	31	0.44	17	0.78	30
1976-77	3.20	100	0.64	20	0.87	27	0.58	18	1.11	35
1977-78	4.29	100	0.96	22	0.91	21	0.56	13	1.86	43
1978-79	4.59	100	1.09	24	0.94	20	0.59	13	1.97	43
1979-80	4.14	100	1.04	25	0.98	24	0.61	15	1.51	36
1980-81	5.10	100	1.22	24	1.19	23	0.73	14	1.96	38
1981-82	5.26	100	1.31	25	1.23	23	0.73	14	1.99	38
1982-83	5.12	100	1.19	23	1.19	23	0.60	12	2.14	42
1983-84	5.82	100	0.98	17	.	.	.	.	.	.

aSource: Table 5.6.
bCalculated from Table 5.6. and Brooks, various issues.
cCosts do not include profits.
dCalculated from Hooks and Kilmer, various issues (b).
eCalculated from Hooks, various issues (b); and Florida Citrus Mutual.
fThis value includes pick and haul and processing firm profits.
gCalculated: On-tree value equals retail value minus f.o.b.-retail margin minus processing cost minus picking and hauling cost.

119

Table 8.7. Proportion of the consumer's retail food dollar spent on 12 46 ounce cans of single strength grapefruit juice that is returned to various marketing channel participants, 1964-65 through 1983-84 seasons.

Season	Retail value[a]	Retail share	F.o.b.-retail margin[b]	F.o.b.-retail margin share	Processing cost[c,d]	Processing cost share	Picking and hauling cost[c,e]	Picking and hauling cost share	On-tree value + marketing firm profit[f,g]	On-tree value + mkt. firm profits share
	$/case	Percent	$/case	Percent	$/case	Percent	$/case	Percent	$/case	Percent
1964-65	4.43	100	1.27	29	1.62	37	0.42	9	1.12	25
1965-66	4.67	100	1.38	30	1.70	36	0.49	10	1.10	24
1966-67	4.03	100	1.34	33	1.68	42	0.46	11	0.55	14
1967-68	4.71	100	1.20	25	1.88	40	0.53	11	1.10	23
1968-69	4.50	100	1.43	32	1.86	41	0.55	12	0.66	15
1969-70	5.42	100	1.36	25	1.98	37	0.58	11	1.50	28
1970-71	5.74	100	1.34	23	2.06	36	0.59	10	1.75	30
1971-72	5.81	100	1.33	23	2.06	35	0.60	10	1.82	31
1972-73	5.60	100	1.48	26	2.16	39	0.68	12	1.28	23
1973-74	5.59	100	1.40	25	2.52	45	0.78	14	0.89	16
1974-75	5.91	100	1.57	27	2.87	49	0.78	13	0.69	12
1975-76	5.90	100	1.51	26	2.82	48	0.78	13	0.79	13
1976-77	6.52	100	1.51	23	2.92	45	0.96	15	1.13	17
1977-78	6.78	100	1.73	26	3.15	46	0.98	14	0.92	14
1978-79	7.62	100	1.58	21	3.49	46	1.02	13	1.53	20
1979-80	9.44	100	2.34	25	3.99	42	1.05	11	2.06	22
1980-81	10.88	100	2.81	26	4.75	44	1.22	11	2.10	19
1981-82	9.95	100	3.45	35	4.89	49	1.12	11	0.49	5
1982-83	9.41	100	3.21	34	4.93	52	1.09	12	0.18	2
1983-84	11.25	100	3.30	29	--	--	--	--	--	--

[a]Florida Department of Citrus, Economic and Market Research Department, various issues.
[b]Calculated from Brooks, various issues.
[c]Costs do not include profits.
[d]Hooks and Kilmer, various issues (b).
[e]Calculated from Hooks, various issues (b); Brooks; and Florida Citrus Mutual.
[f]This value includes pick and haul and processing firm profits.
[g]Calculated: On-tree value equals retail value minus f.o.b.-retail margin minus processing cost minus picking and hauling cost.

retail price paid for orange concentrate in six-ounce cans. The f.o.b. retail and processing costs have both averaged 25 percent. Picking and hauling costs have accounted for the lowest percentage of the retail dollar (15 percent).

For canned grapefruit juice the relative proportion of the retail dollar to processing costs is higher than for concentrate (43 compared to 25 percent) (Tables 8.6 and 8.7). Picking and hauling costs represent a lower percentage of the retail dollar (12 percent) while on-tree value plus marketing firm profits are 19 percent and have the highest coefficient of variation (42.5 percent). The f.o.b. retail margin is approximately 27 percent of the retail dollar and shows a higher coefficient of variation than processing costs (14.41 percent compared to 12.04 percent).

The f.o.b. retail margin for fresh grapefruit accounted for 62 percent of the retail food dollar for the past 20 seasons (Table 8.5). For every dollar a consumer has spent on fresh grapefruit, 62 cents pays for services that occur after it leaves Florida packinghouses. Picking, hauling, packing, and selling expenses account for 20 cents and on-tree value plus marketing firm profits are 18 cents. On-tree returns displayed the highest coefficient of variation at 20.94 percent while the f.o.b. retail margin share, the packing cost share, and the picking and hauling cost share had coefficients of 6.05, 6.25, and 8.49 percent, which shows a lower variability than on-tree returns.

U.S. Citrus Industry Gross Revenues

The total estimated final consumer value of oranges and grapefruit (fresh and processed) from Florida peaked in 1979–80 at $3.1 billion and has not returned to that level (Table 8.8). The freezes in Florida have decreased the quantity of citrus marketed. Processed citrus sales represented 71 percent of the total, and fresh citrus accounted for the remaining portion in 1983–84.

The total on-tree U.S. industry value is available (Table 8.9). Note specifically that Florida citrus accounts for 65.1 percent of the total on-tree value and that 49.9 percent of the total U.S. industry value is from processed Florida usages in 1985–86. California, Texas, and Arizona accounted for 32.4, 0.5 and 2.0 percent of the total on-tree value in 1985–86.

The percentage of the citrus retail dollar claimed by each level of the vertical market system differs between processed and fresh products (Table 8.10). The retail-f.o.b. processing plant price spread for processed citrus is approximately 20 percent of the retail price compared to 60

Table 8.8   Estimated final consumer value of the Florida orange and grapefruit sector, 1970-71 through 1983-84.

Year	Fresh citrus[a]	Processed citrus[b]	Total
1970-71	$376,800,720[c]	$ 801,902,290[f]	$1,178,703,101
1971-72	401,311,520[c]	924,691,730[f]	1,326,003,250
1972-73	440,919,720[c]	1,090,789,610[f]	1,531,709,330
1973-74	476,493,420[c]	1,007,744,320[f]	1,554,237,740
1974-75	521,026,540[c]	1,195,297,380	1,716,323,920
1975-76	526,863,780[c]	1,291,431,080	1,818,294,860
1976-77	431,822,560[c]	1,344,669,600	1,776,492,200
1977-78	-- [d]	1,801,139,800	--
1978-79	-- [d]	2,043,691,500	--
1979-80	755,588,430[e]	2,359,969,000	3,115,557,400
1980-81	644,786,480[e]	2,249,957,400	2,894,743,900
1981-82	637,588,440[e]	1,854,755,300	2,492,343,700
1982-83	778,649,940[e]	2,046,736,500	2,825,386,400
1983-84	690,973,560[e]	1,718,748,200	2,409,721,800

Note: The estimated final consumer value is calculated using retail prices for fresh and processed products. The unknown quantity of products used by institutions and the quantity of product exported are valued at retail prices.
[a]The quantities of oranges and grapefruit used are the Florida packinghouse utilization of citrus grove fruit (Florida Citrus Mutual).
[b]Orange and grapefruit processed products considered are concentrate, chilled single strength, and canned single strength juice. The product quantities are the Florida processing plant utilization of citrus grove fruit (Florida Citrus Mutual). The retail prices are from the Florida Department of Citrus, Economic and Market Research Department.
[c]The price used is a weighted average retail price from four cities--Atlanta, Boston, Chicago, Pittsburgh (USDA unpublished data).
[d]Price data was not available.
[e]The price used is a weighted average retail price from two cities--Baltimore and Boston (USDA unpublished data).
[f]Chilled single strength grapefruit juice is not included for lack of data.

Table 8.9.   On-tree value ($1,000) of fresh and processed oranges and grapefruit for the United States and various states, 1971-72 through 1985-86.

	Oranges			Grapefruit		
	Fresh	Processed	Total	Fresh	Processed	Total
United States						
1971-72	$115,733	$259,373	$375,106	$82,134	$60,895	$143,029
1972-73	133,959	248,325	382,284	81,150	49,187	130,337
1973-74	143,705	221,759	365,464	68,636	36,631	105,267
1974-75	165,171	243,774	408,945	83,943	21,482	105,425
1975-76	137,694	290,796	428,490	75,198	22,976	98,174
1976-77	155,243	383,324	538,567	70,477	40,799	111,276
1977-78	266,697	659,307	926,004	74,228	41,572	115,800
1978-79	269,176	721,193	990,369	100,470	57,453	157,923
1979-80	208,828	727,797	936,625	114,536	105,208	219,744
1980-81	272,097	645,475	917,572	143,221	94,341	237,562
1981-82	379,921	492,612	872,533	113,282	27,434	140,716
1982-83	275,767	658,804	934,571	102,169	6,303	108,472
1983-84	403,565	604,464	1,008,029	107,629	36,263	143,865
1984-85	496,610	679,374	1,175,984	147,888	75,593	223,481
1985-86	346,618	391,034	737,652	161,507	81,931	243,438

122

Table 8.9. (continued).

	Oranges			Grapefruit		
	Fresh	Processed	Total	Fresh	Processed	Total

Florida

1971-72	$28,134	$252,183	$280,317	$53,453	$55,538	$108,991
1972-73	22,645	242,716	265,361	52,910	41,725	94,635
1973-74	23,293	221,398	244,691	47,478	32,401	79,879
1974-75	28,196	252,154	280,350	57,003	19,364	76,367
1975-76	26,392	295,057	321,449	50,651	21,504	72,155
1976-77	19,593	386,389	405,982	42,382	38,734	81,116
1977-78	48,373	645,304	693,677	42,224	42,214	84,438
1978-79	62,727	702,234	764,961	63,596	56,532	120,128
1979-80	45,720	723,157	768,877	80,422	100,786	181,208
1980-81	47,927	649,304	697,231	89,695	91,460	181,155
1981-82	49,621	489,065	538,686	74,846	25,751	100,597
1982-83	61,273	657,147	718,420	66,195	11,026	77,221
1983-84	59,245	611,373	670,618	69,894	41,264	111,158
1984-85	73,911	664,012	737,923	84,208	77,148	161,356
1985-86	47,446	405,636	453,082	101,732	83,890	185,622

California

1971-72	$77,253	$1,557	$78,810	$12,426	$884	$13,310
1972-73	96,331	292	96,623	10,886	409	11,295
1973-74	111,615	-3,915	107,700	8,189	488	8,677
1974-75	124,932	-9,944	114,588	11,356	-406	10,950
1975-76	102,604	-7,866	94,738	9,547	-393	9,154
1976-77	122,480	-8,379	114,101	12,325	-1,690	10,635
1977-78	193,592	3,450	197,042	21,312	-2,596	18,716
1978-79	187,346	4,475	191,821	24,317	-1,635	22,682
1979-80	147,608	-1,996	145,612	15,570	-1,939	13,631
1980-81	205,507	-7,710	197,797	28,465	-1,615	26,850
1981-82	303,792	-5,000	298,792	14,635	-3,203	11,432
1982-83	189,097	-5,186	183,911	17,901	-3,773	14,128
1983-84	327,701	-9,886	317,815	24,469	-4,008	20,461
1984-85	404,262	14,724	418,986	50,732	-1,156	49,576
1985-86	284,132	-14,190	269,942	49,272	-1,462	47,810

Texas

1971-72	$4,758	$4,658	$9,416	$12,858	$4,221	$17,079
1972-73	4,295	4,549	8,844	14,582	6,607	21,189
1973-74	3,072	4,368	7,440	10,368	3,604	13,972
1974-75	4,507	2,130	6,637	11,858	2,385	14,243
1975-76	4,959	3,866	8,825	12,577	1,955	14,532
1976-77	7,025	6,003	13,028	12,182	4,381	16,563
1977-78	10,556	9,991	20,547	8,052	3,286	11,338
1978-79	8,148	3,287	21,435	8,000	3,300	11,300
1979-80	9,714	6,415	16,129	13,356	7,067	20,423
1980-81	11,758	4,537	16,295	17,205	4,736	21,941
1981-82	13,320	8,595	21,915	19,738	6,537	26,275
1982-83	13,894	6,656	20,750	13,650	476	14,126
1983-84	5,699	3,024	8,723	6,406	82	6,488
1984-85	0	0	0	0	0	0
1985-86	2,694	80	2,774	1,786	71	1,857

123

Table 8.9. (continued).

	Oranges			Grapefruit		
	Fresh	Processed	Total	Fresh	Processed	Total
			Arizona			
1971-72	$5,588	$975	$6,563	$3,397	$252	$3,649
1972-73	10,688	768	11,456	2,772	446	3,218
1973-74	5,725	-92	5,633	2,601	138	2,739
1974-75	7,936	-566	7,370	3,726	139	3,865
1975-76	3,739	-261	3,478	2,423	-90	2,333
1976-77	6,145	-689	5,456	3,588	-626	2,962
1977-78	14,176	562	14,738	2,640	-1,332	1,308
1978-79	10,955	1,197	12,152	4,557	-744	3,813
1979-80	5,786	221	6,007	5,188	-706	4,482
1980-81	6,905	-656	6,249	7,856	-240	7,616
1981-82	13,188	-48	13,140	4,063	-1,651	2,412
1982-83	11,503	-13	11,490	4,423	-1,426	2,997
1983-84	10,920	-47	10,873	6,860	-1,102	5,758
1984-85	18,437	638	19,075	12,948	-399	12,549
1985-86	12,346	-492	11,854	8,717	-568	8,149

Source: Florida Crop and Livestock Reporting Service, various issues.

percent for fresh citrus. Much of the difference between these spreads is due to the fact that fresh citrus is extremely bulky and perishable; this increases the transportation, handling, and storage costs.

Product transformation to processed products is more costly than grading and packaging fresh citrus. Picking, hauling, and processing accounted for 51 percent of the estimated final consumer dollar for processed products in 1983–84 up from 46 percent the previous year (Table 8.10). The percentages have been cyclical and are returning to 1974–75 levels. On the other hand, fresh citrus picking, hauling, and packing accounted for only 20 percent of the retail citrus dollar in 1983–84, an amount that has been reasonably stable since 1971. In fact, the price spread at each level as a percentage of the retail price is relatively more stable in fresh citrus than processed (Table 8.10).

Finally, the grove cost expressed as a percentage of on-tree returns is significantly higher for processed as compared to fresh citrus (Table 8.11). Citrus sold fresh generated net returns that were higher per 1⅗ bushel box than citrus used in processing. The on-tree price is derived by subtracting picking, hauling, and packing costs from an average f.o.b. packinghouse price for fresh citrus, and profits are not included in these costs. The on-tree prices derived for fresh citrus include packinghouse and picking and hauling profits, which slightly inflates the on-tree net returns to fresh citrus. The on-tree price derived for processed citrus includes the profits of pick and haul firms, which slightly inflates the on-tree price.

Table 8.10. Percentage and dollars of the estimated final consumer dollar claimed by different levels of the vertical market of Florida citrus, 1970-71 through 1983-84.

Year	Producer level		Processor and packinghouse level		Wholesale-retail distribution level	
	Processed[a]	Fresh[b]	Processed[c]	Fresh[d]	Processed[e]	Fresh[e]
1970-71	27%	18%	48%	21%	24%	61%
	($219,706)	($65,922)	($386,223)	($ 80,199)	($195,973)	($230,678)
1971-72	34%	21%	42%	19%	24%	60%
	($311,051)	($86,398)	($391,473)	($ 75,549)	($222,169)	($239,364)
1972-73	26%	18%	46%	20%	27%	62%
	($283,403)	($79,978)	($509,928)	($ 89,374)	($297,459)	($271,567)
1973-74	24%	16%	51%	20%	25%	64%
	($255,948)	($74,908)	($554,349)	($ 95,244)	($267,447)	($306,341)
1974-75	23%	17%	53%	21%	23%	62%
	($277,302)	($89,240)	($640,207)	($109,564)	($277,789)	($322,223)
1975-76	25%	16%	51%	22%	24%	62%
	($323,310)	($82,226)	($658,876)	($116,939)	($309,245)	($327,699)
1976-77	32%	16%	47%	21%	21%	63%
	($430,796)	($64,758)	($632,055)	($ 89,485)	($281,819)	($266,244)
1977-78	39%	--	38%	--	23%	--
	($707,349)	($100,698)	($677,691)	($120,378)	($416,100)	--
1978-79	38%	--	37%	--	25%	--
	($780,352)	($138,286)	($760,198)	($153,938)	($503,142)	--
1979-80	36%	18%	41%	21%	23%	61%
	($848,927)	($138,445)	($974,575)	($158,272)	($536,467)	($458,871)
1980-81	34%	22%	43%	20%	23%	58%
	($758,114)	($144,605)	($967,019)	($129,369)	($524,824)	($370,812)
1981-82	29%	21%	47%	19%	24%	60%
	($540,438)	($130,596)	($869,367)	($123,191)	($444,950)	($383,801)
1982-83	34%	18%	46%	21%	20%	61%
	($693,853)	($136,944)	($940,747)	($164,512)	($412,137)	($477,194)
1983-84	32%	20%	51%	20%	17%	60%
	($552,290)	($137,079)	($882,367)	($141,352)	($284,091)	($412,543)

[a]Orange and grapefruit processed products considered are concentrate, chilled single strength, and canned single strength juice. The product quantities are the Florida processing plant utilization of citrus grove fruit from Florida Citrus Mutual. The price used is the processed product on-tree price (Florida Crop and Livestock Reporting Service).

[b]The quantities of fresh oranges and grapefruit used are the Florida packinghouse utilization of citrus grove fruit from Florida Citrus Mutual. The price used is the fresh product on-tree price (Florida Crop and Livestock Reporting Service).

[c]Orange and grapefruit processed products and quantity data sources are stated in footnote a. The f.o.b. prices used are for 12 6 ounce FCOJ; 12 32 ounce COJ; 12 46 ounce CSSOJ; 12 6 ounce FCGJ; 12 32 ounce CGJ; 12 46 ounce CSSGJ from Brooks. The average number of gallons per 1 3/5 bushel box is from Florida Citrus Mutual. The processed value is determined by subtracting the f.o.b. value from the producer level value (processed).

[d]The data source for fresh oranges and grapefruit quantities is stated in footnote b. The f.o.b. price data is from Growers Administrative Committee. The fresh value is determined by subtracting the f.o.b. value from the producer level value (fresh).

[e]These values are calculated by subtracting the processed (fresh) retail value in Table 8.8 from the f.o.b. processed (fresh) value for the processor and packinghouse level shown in this table.

Table 8.11   Estimated total cost as a percentage of estimated total revenue at the Florida grower level, 1974-75 through 1983-84.

Year	Producer level[a] Processed	Fresh
	%	%
1974-75	72	54
1975-76	64	50
1976-77	51	50
1977-78	33	28
1978-79	33	28
1979-80	37	33
1980-81	45	31
1981-82	61	39
1982-83	46	39
1983-84	62	37

[a]Percentage calculated by grove cost divided by on-tree value times 100. Grove cost from Figure 8.1. On-tree fresh use price from Figure 5.1a. On-tree processed use price from Florida Crop and Livestock Reporting Service, various issues.

Losses in the Citrus Industry.   Both oranges and grapefruit are fully utilized. As oranges enter the packinghouse and are rejected, eliminations are diverted to processing plants. Once at the processor, each orange and grapefruit is individually squeezed. In one operation the juices are extracted, pulp is separated from the fruit, and citrus oils are processed from the rind. The pulp and rind go together to make a citrus feed. The citrus industry has made considerable improvement in its technology in order to utilize all parts of citrus for processing. Little waste is evident, and spoilage is at a minimum.

IV

International
Trade

9

Citrus Trade
and the
U.S. Domestic
Markets

Of all economic events influencing the U.S. citrus industry, the growth of the Brazilian production of oranges has been the most dramatic. As noted in earlier chapters, Brazil's production has surpassed U.S. production in the last several years and nearly all of Brazil's processed citrus is exported, with the major portion entering the U.S. markets. Similarly, Brazil's trade with other markets such as Canada and the European Economic Community (EEC) directly competes with U.S. attempts to expand its foreign markets for processed citrus products. In this chapter trade activities are analyzed as they relate to growth of the U.S. markets for citrus products and their subsequent effects on U.S. imports and exports. Before proceeding it is again useful to highlight the general characteristics of the product and how it is used.

Both Brazilian and U.S. involvement in international citrus trade is primarily in the form of processed citrus products. Brazil almost exclusively exports bulk frozen concentrated orange juice. This juice, much like many manufacturing products, must be transformed into a consumable good. In particular, bulk concentrate must be reconstituted into either retail quality frozen concentrate or into ready-to-serve orange juice. During much of the seventies and early eighties the quality or grade of Brazilian juice was such that it could only be used if blended with U.S. domestically produced orange juices. The product grades were generally below the minimum necessary to directly reconstitute the Brazilian juice into consumable forms. However, as the Brazilian industry matured, so did the quality and grades of its orange concentrate. Much

129

of the imported Brazilian concentrate can now be directly reconstituted without blending with product from Florida or other domestic sources. Also, in several seasons Florida processors were forced to import Brazilian juices in order to meet minimum color requirements for early season processing. Most of the imports into Florida in the early seventies were for this purpose.

A second major change has been with the growth of bulk shipping and storage. Through most of the seventies concentrate was stored and shipped in 55 gallon drums. This created considerable inefficiencies in terms of shipping costs, distribution, inspection, and reconstitution. Large orange juice tank farms are now the predominant storage method for most processors. Similarly, an increasing share of imported concentrate is shipped in large bulk tankers much in the same style as petroleum. These tankers enter specific U.S. ports and the juice is off-loaded into the tank farm facilities and then subsequently distributed to recon-operations such as large dairy processing facilities.

U.S. Imports of FCOJ

Figures 9.1 and 9.2 illustrate well the dynamics of international trade in frozen concentrated orange juice. FCOJ exports from the United States started to decline in 1981 and decreased 50 percent by 1986. FCOJ imports showed continued growth throughout the seventies, but after 1980 imports increased fivefold. Much of this latter growth can be at least in part attributed to the fact that Florida experienced four major freezes in 1981, 1982, 1983, and 1985. During this same period, imports increased from under 100 million gallons of single strength equivalent juice to over 500 million gallons in 1985. (Recall that the single strength equivalent gallon is approximately equal to ¼ gallon of frozen concentrate expressed in 42 degrees brixs, which is what is typical on the grocery shelf.)

Figure 9.2 puts these imports into perspective with domestic production. First, the notable loss in domestic supplies is clearly seen in this graph with the declines in Florida pack after 1980. Imports filled the supply gap created by the freeze losses and by 1986 over 50 percent of the U.S. supplies were imported. Total supplies rose along with the increase in the Brazilian share of the U.S. market.

These imports have obviously had a profound impact on the U.S. orange industry. Without these foreign supplies the domestic industry would have suffered considerably. Orange juice prices would have been high enough to possibly force consumers out of the market or force them

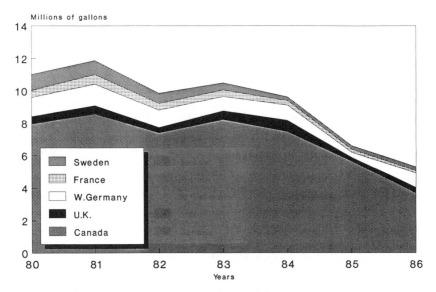

Figure 9.1. U.S. exports of frozen concentrated orange juice.

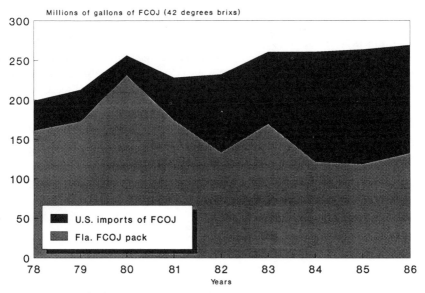

Figure 9.2. U.S. supplies of frozen orange concentrate by source.

to switch to other juices and/or artificial substitutes. Losses of citrus fruit leaves the processing industry with considerable excess capacity. Imports can be used in conjunction with domestic supplies to operate plants at lower per unit costs. This is a major reason why several Florida processors have been actively involved in the import of frozen concentrate.

While imports lead to major benefits to both processors and consumers in terms of pricing and efficiency, they have also led to significant structural changes within the domestic markets. Florida is no longer the primary supplier of orange juice to the U.S. markets. The ability of a few Florida processors to exercise price leadership is no longer possible (or has been limited) simply because buyers of concentrate now have an alternative to the domestic supplies. One could argue that consumer welfare, as measured with consumer surplus, should have increased dramatically with this structural change. A possible cost to the consumer may be felt through a wider variety of product qualities. The Florida industry has maintained rigid quality standards for product packaged within the state and then shipped commercially. Florida standards have historically exceeded federal levels. This possibility is not due solely to the availability of imports, however. For several years there has been an increasing trend toward Florida processors shipping bulk concentrate out of state for later reconstitution at points nearer the consuming centers. Florida standards no longer apply to the out-of-state reprocessing of the bulk juices.

At the current state of development, orange concentrate enters the U.S. markets in bulk form. There is little to no effort put forth by Brazil and other suppliers to establish an identity for their juice. Most is simply reconstituted, with the final product carrying a brand label of the firm doing the reprocessing or the private label for particular retail food chains. The supply source in terms of the consumer's perception is not emphasized for these imports. Product identity is a major issue among Florida producers as is discussed in Chapter 7. At this point it is sufficient to note that the Florida citrus industry has maintained a product identity label emphasizing that certain juices meet Florida's minimum standards as illustrated by the Florida standards label on those packages meeting the criteria of standards and sources.

COJ Consumption and Imports

Imports of bulk concentrate enter the U.S. markets and are, for the most part, reconstituted into ready-to-serve orange juice (or chilled orange juices). Current data sources do not track these juices through the complete market chain until they reach the final consumer. Thus it is impossible to completely identify the utilization of imported juices except to note that most enter the ready-to-serve market. Furthermore, one cannot at any point in time exactly determine the percentage of chilled orange juice in the U.S. market being supplied from foreign sources.

Figure 9.3 provides some insight into the complexity of trying to trace the source of chilled supplies. Each bar in this figure represents the annual total chilled retail market in the United States as reported by Nielsen Marketing Service. These data are calculated from samples of store audits and then projected to the total United States and they have proven quite accurate over time. The dark portion of each bar reports ready-to-serve orange juice that was processed, packaged, and shipped from Florida. The upper values reflect chilled juices packaged outside of Florida. As apparent for the years beyond 1981, nearly one-third or more of the U.S. supplies are from non-Florida packed juices. A large portion of these other supplies must be from imported juices. Yet one cannot immediately assume that, for example in 1986, imports ac-

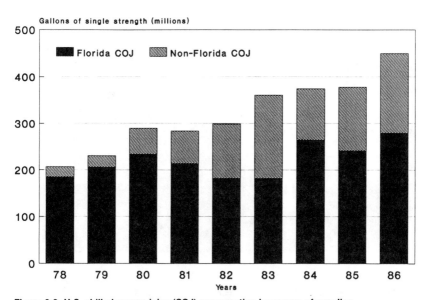

Figure 9.3. U.S. chilled orange juice (COJ) consumption by source of supplies.

counted for nearly 40 percent of the ready-to-serve market. First, Florida processors imported concentrate, some portion of which is included in shipments shown in the lower parts of each bar. Second, Florida exports bulk concentrate that is later reprocessed. Hence, a share of the upper graph includes reconstituted Florida juice and a portion of the lower bar includes imports. It simply is impossible to precisely determine the relative shares of the chilled market supplied by foreign versus domestic juices. Probably the index of relative importance is best shown with Figure 9.2.

Ports of Entry for FCOJ

The Department of Commerce maintains detailed data on imports of frozen concentrate in all U.S. ports. New York, Delaware, Los Angeles, and Tampa account for most imports. While data on individual ports are of interest, the most important trend is illustrated with Figure 9.4. In 1978 nearly 83 percent of all orange concentrate imports entered the U.S. through Florida ports. By 1986 this had shifted so that Florida accounted for only 46 percent of total imports. This trend reflects the

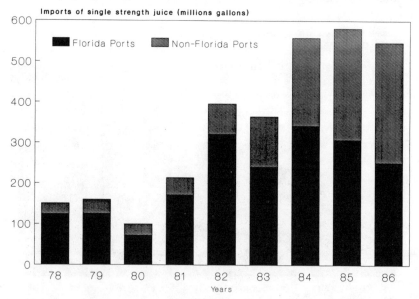

Figure 9.4. U.S. imports of frozen orange concentrate according to the port of entry.

growth in large tank farms outside of Florida nearer to major consuming areas in the Atlantic states and in California. These percentages are further reflective of the structural shift where Florida processors have less control over pricing policies, standards, and distribution practices. These shifts are likely to be permanent since they include an underlying capital investment in receiving and storage facilities and reconstitution operations.

Import Price Patterns

During the early seventies U.S. concentrate prices provided the leading index for concentrate on which all other processed citrus exports were based. While the Florida price is still an important indication of citrus value, both the Florida and Brazilian prices are now determined simultaneously. That is, both prices are interdependent rather than Florida's price being the leading index. This evolved as Brazil increased its share of the world's markets. While previous trade statistics have been expressed in gallons of concentrate (either single strength or in processed retail pack concentrate of 42 degrees brixs), most prices are expressed in pounds of orange solids or in metric tons. All volume units, whether in single strength or concentrate, can be easily converted to pounds of orange solids.

Figure 9.5 shows the relative prices for Florida and Brazilian orange concentrate expressed in equivalent pounds of solids. The Florida price is f.o.b. for the U.S. markets and Brazil's price excludes shipping costs, tariffs, and related import taxes. Imports of orange concentrate into the United States are presently subject to a 34 cents per pound of solids tariff. Furthermore, imports brought into Florida are subject to an additional 3 cents equalization tax designed to align Brazilian price because of governmental subsidies the Brazilian government provides to its orange processing industry. The price differential showing the difference between Florida and Brazilian prices reflects in part these real costs associated with importing of foreign juices. Note in this figure the difference averages around 48 cents per pound of orange solids, reflecting mostly the costs of shipping, tariffs, and taxes. Also, the peak prices seen in 1981, 1982, and 1984 reflect the effects of several Florida freezes that occurred in those years.

There exists a strong relationship between the levels of imports (Figure 9.2) and the prices shown in Figure 9.5. Specifically, as the price spread between Florida and Brazil increases, there should be a substantial increase in imports of concentrate. Ward (1977) established this rela-

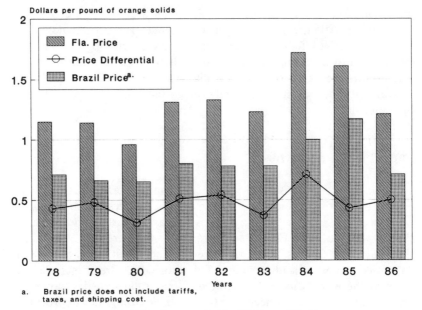

Dollars per pound of orange solids

a. Brazil price does not include tariffs, taxes, and shipping cost.

Figure 9.5. Comparison of FCOJ prices reported for Florida and Brazil.

tionship prior to the major influx of Brazilian juices when he showed that imports increase exponentially with a rise in the price spread. Subsequent analysis for the latter periods further confirms these earlier findings once the major growth in the eighties has been considered.

Table 9.1 shows a simple regression between the imports of concentrate, price differences, and a growth trend variable. The growth variable defined simply as a yearly trend (i.e., YR = 78, 79, . . .) provides a proxy for the significant imports occurring in the eighties. Furthermore, reported imports and the average prices shown in Figure 9.5 may not exactly correspond since some imports purchased have been bought forward or early in the seasons, possibly priced off of the futures market. Prior seasons' prices may have a partial effect on current imports simply because of the potential accounting problems where the yearly price may not exactly match up with the imported value. Therefore, a lagged price difference is also included in the import equation.

As most apparent in Table 9.1, both the current year average difference and last year differential have significant effects on imports. Both parameters in this table can be interpreted as import elasticities such that a 10 percent increase in the price difference can be expected to lead to a 13.4 percent increase in imports. If the differential increase

Table 9.1. Relationship between imports of frozen orange concentrate into the U.S. and the spread between Florida and Brazil concentrate price.

Variable	Coefficient	Std. error	T-Stat.	2-Tail Sig.
C	-57.915378	12.114838	-4.7805325	0.009
LDIF	1.3422525	0.3452283	3.8880141	0.018
LDIF(-1)	0.8114868	0.3451186	2.3513274	0.078
LYR	14.486073	2.6817211	5.4017820	0.006

R-squared	0.960622	Mean of dependent var	4.354092
Adjusted R-squared	0.931088	S.D. of dependent var	0.655071
S.E. of regression	0.171964	Sum of squared resid	0.118286
Durbin-Watson stat	2.028834	F-statistic	32.52616
Log likelihood	5.504862		

Dependent variable is LIMP or Log of Imports (in gallons of 42 dg. bx).
SMPL range: 1979-1986
Number of observations: 8

persists, say at 10 percent, then the imports would be expected to increase by 21.5 percent. Clearly, imports are increasing at an exponential rate with a rising price spread. Some apparent conditions that could change the meaning of the current differential and its effect on imports would include an adjustment in the tariff schedule, rising shipping cost, imposition of additional taxes, all of which lessen the potential gains from the widening differential. The year trend variable is simply capturing the growth during the periods in which Florida experienced large crop losses. While imports may continue to increase, the growth shown in these results may not be representative of future periods. However, the price relationship should continue to be valid.

U.S. Exports of Orange Juices

U.S. exports of orange juices generally account for less than 10 percent of the total domestic supplies. Between 1980 and 1986 total exports declined almost proportionally with total domestic supplies as illustrated in Figure 9.6. Much of this decline is directly related to rising FCOJ prices in markets that are considerably more elastic than the U.S. domestic market. Ward showed the EEC market for concentrate to have an elasticity of approximately 2.26 compared to the domestic level of 0.52. Hence rising prices in such elastic markets would assuredly lead to substantial reductions in consumption.

Exports in millions gallons (42 degrees brixs)

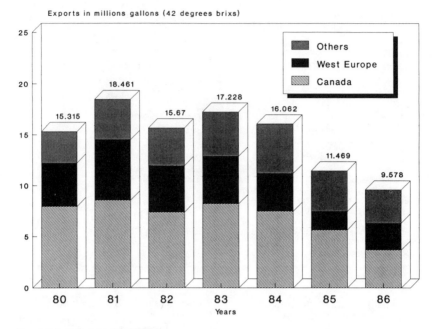

Figure 9.6. U.S. exports of FCOJ.

Canada has been the major purchaser of U.S. orange concentrate, with approximately 50 percent of all U.S. exports going to that market. However, by 1986 this percentage dropped to nearer 40 percent. Recent data show Canada importing an increasing amount from Brazil. The EEC generally accounts for 25 percent of U.S. exports, with West Germany being the largest importer among the EEC members. Other markets account for the remainder and this percentage has increased from around 20 percent to 30 percent in the more recent periods. These percentage shifts are likely permanent given Canada's increasing rates of imports from Brazil.

The U.S. has maintained several programs directed at developing the foreign markets for foreign concentrate. Quality control and packaging innovations have been an ongoing effort. Furthermore, joint promotional efforts between Florida, the U.S. Foreign Agricultural Service, and foreign distribution have been carried out for several years. These efforts are commonly referred to as three-party programs where each party contributes a share to promoting Florida citrus in the importing market. Generally, the contributions are 30 percent each by Florida and FAS and 40 percent by the foreign distributor. Studies by Lee (1977) and by Myers (1979) have shown these programs to be successful in generating additional foreign sales of Florida concentrate.

Both in real and absolute terms, expenditures on the Three Party Program have declined substantially in the last several years. Peak expenditures occurred in 1973, when Florida spent approximately $800,000 with the bulk of these funds going to Sweden and West Germany. Levels ranged from $600,000 to $800,000 between 1973 and 1983, but after 1982 Florida contributions to the program dropped to around $250,000. Again, this decline is reflective of the loss of support funds due to the reduction in supplies from which taxes used to support these programs are collected. As the industry recovers from the crop losses of the early eighties, it is likely and probably essential that these programs be once again strongly supported.

Another program designed to encourage processors to develop their foreign markets has been the Duty Drawback Program. If a processor or importer exports a given quantity of concentrate within a three-year period, then duties paid on any imports of like concentrate in that same period can be regained or "drawn back," thus giving the name "Duty Drawback." Early emphasis for this program arose out of the need to import concentrate for blending purposes and for providing a source of cheaper concentrate that could be used to establish a two-pricing system for Florida suppliers. The two prices would allow for cheaper export prices for the more elastic foreign markets and a higher domestic price in the more inelastic market. The blending of foreign and domestic sources would allow for lower export prices without cutting prices paid back to producers for domestic supplies. The drawback provisions then encouraged the development of export markets in order to regain the substantial duties paid. In many seasons these duties accounted for 33 to nearly 50 percent of the value of the imported juice.

Given the significant increase in imports and the reduction in U.S. exports of orange juices, the duty drawback programs have less impact on the total trade situation. Concentrate prices during the eighties were so high that processors had little motivation for supporting a two-pricing system, since almost all domestic supplies could be readily sold in the U.S. markets. Less emphasis on exports and other secondary markets during periods of domestic shortages is a logical outcome when the trade is faced with more elastic secondary markets.

U.S. Fresh Citrus Trade

Both oranges and grapefruit are exported as fresh fruit as shown in Figures 9.7 and 9.8. Total U.S. fresh oranges have ranges between 48 to 60 million boxes in the eighties with approximately 10 million being exported. As is apparent in Figure 9.7, exports have changed very little in the last several seasons when compared to total fresh supplies. In terms of distribution, over 50 percent of these exports are to Hong Kong and Japan and around 25 percent to Canada. European consumption of U.S. fresh oranges is insignificant.

Export markets for fresh grapefruit have taken on increasing importance in the last decade with the more important increase seen in the Japanese markets. Figure 9.8 shows these grapefruit exports relative to total U.S. fresh supplies, with exports in the latter years ranging near the seven million box level. Japan accounted for nearly 50 percent of these exports, while France and the Netherlands imported roughly 25 percent. A study by Ward and Tang (1978, 83–88) showed the demands for fresh grapefruit to differ across these markets where the U.S. demand elasticity was estimated to be −0.74; Canadian elasticity, −1.25; Japan, −3.57; and the EEC elasticity at −0.34. Since that study, it is most likely that the elasticities have changed and especially so for the Japanese market.

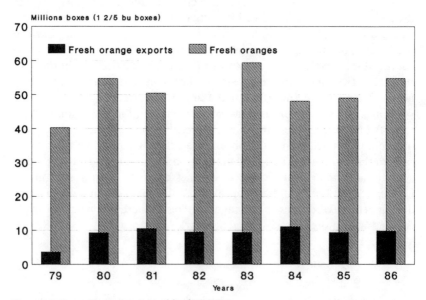

Figure 9.7. Domestic and exports of fresh oranges.

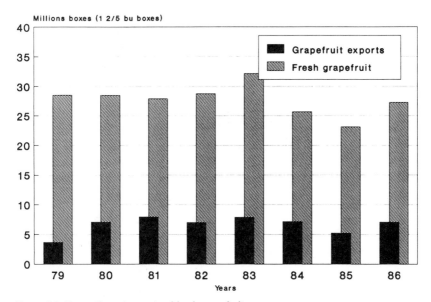

Figure 9.8. Domestic and exports of fresh grapefruit.

In summary, the U.S. processed orange industry is domestically oriented with the Canadian market being the largest importer. Imports into the U.S. market are expected to continue to grow, especially given the major changes in port facilities that have taken place in the last several years and with rising demand for chilled orange juice. Brazil will remain a major factor in the U.S. markets for orange juice. Structural changes among Florida processors have already occurred, primarily in terms of price leadership, procurement practices, and processing forms. More chilled orange juice will be processed out of the state of Florida by firms not directly affiliated with the Florida processing industry. In the near future it is also likely that significant changes in the efforts to support and promote generic advertising in the U.S. will occur. Currently, U.S. and predominantly Florida producers provide the support for national generic advertising of processed citrus. Yet over half of the chilled market is supplied by imported concentrate and a major share of this is not subject to the taxes supporting generic advertising. Either this tax structure must change or the advertising must be much more focused to product identity. Given the homogeneous nature of orange juice, it is probably impossible to establish real differences in product between Florida and other sources.

10

International
Markets

The Institutional Structure for Trade

The world's citrus trade takes place in a complex economic market-place of competing suppliers selling both fresh and processed citrus. Citrus including oranges, grapefruit, and lemons is produced worldwide, yet only a few countries provide nearly all of the commercial export supplies. Most of the larger producing countries depend on foreign markets for a share of their citrus sales.

During the last two decades, processed citrus in the forms of frozen concentrate and single strength juices has gained increasing consumer acceptance. As production and marketing of processed citrus continues to grow, storage decisions become an increasingly important dimension to the producing countries. Also each supplying country faces the economic issues relating to market development. How such problems are addressed differs considerably among the supplying countries.

Figures 10.1 and 10.2 illustrate the growth in citrus production by major countries and by type. Prior to the midseventies the United States supplied approximately 33 percent of the total world's production of oranges. During these years Brazil's production represented less than 14 percent of the world total as shown with the middle area in Figure 10.1. Major plantings and increased productivity led to significant growth in the Brazilian industry in the late seventies. By 1983 the U.S. and Brazil share of the total world production was nearly equal. Subsequent freezes in Florida reduced Florida's crop size and Brazil became the largest

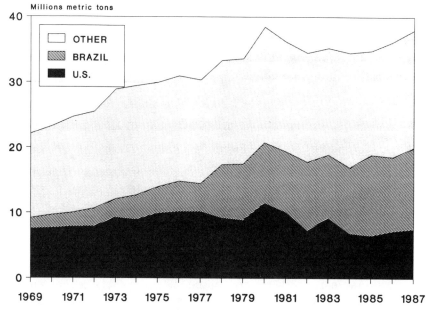

Figure 10.1. World production of oranges.

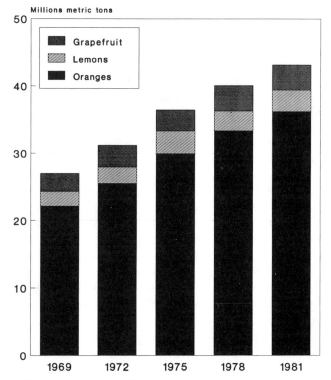

Figure 10.2. Citrus production according to type.

world supplier of oranges. In 1987 Brazil accounted for around 33 percent of the total while the United States contributed nearly 20 percent. These two countries combined produced 53 percent of the world's commercial supplies of oranges. Note in Figure 10.1 that most of the share shifting has been between the United States and Brazil. The total share of all remaining countries has remained nearly constant since the mid-seventies.

Most of the text has been devoted to the orange industry because of its importance relative to the other major citrus products. In Figure 10.2 the size of orange production worldwide relative to lemon and grapefruit is shown. Since 1969 orange production has consistently accounted for around 82 to 84 percent of the total citrus supplies. The proportion between oranges, lemons, and grapefruit has remained relatively constant with the growth in total production.

The evolution of citrus trade is not unlike many of the world's agricultural markets. There are consuming regions that cannot supply domestic demands and producing regions having a comparative advantage in the production and marketing of selected agricultural products. Comparative advantage simply means that one producing region may have some economic advantage over a competing supplier. Geographic and natural resource differences among countries can clearly lead to production advantages of one or more supplying regions. For example, Spain has a geographical advantage for supplying fresh oranges to the European markets. Spain's economic trade access to the European markets has been further advanced with its membership in the European Economic Community (EEC). Economic trade advantages will evolve out of the different institutional structures found among importing and exporting countries. The infrastructure of supplying regions directly impacts each country's ability to compete in world markets and to supply domestic demands. Likewise, the market and political infrastructures of the major importing countries may be designed to favor one source of supplies over another. To understand citrus economics one must have a clear picture of those institutions and organizations that direct the flow of citrus from production to final consumption, whether this takes place within one country's boundaries or across boundaries such as with the EEC. The task at hand then is to identify the economic systems in place that impact citrus trade and try to make some judgment about the economic consequences of specific institutional arrangements. It is essential to keep in perspective the types of controls particular organizations have on the buying and selling functions.

In the following discussions we will first identify which countries are the major suppliers and briefly show how they utilize their production. Common economic issues are discussed and then the range of institutional structures found among the major producers is shown.

Major Citrus Producers.   Before identifying those specific institutions that facilitate the functioning of the world's citrus industries, it is essential that the major producers are recognized. Both the volume of production and the levels of utilization for fresh versus processed and domestic consumption versus exports lead to significant differences among the larger producing countries.

During the eighties the largest producing countries included the United States, Brazil, Japan, Spain, Italy, Israel, Egypt, South Africa, and Morocco and accounted for over 70 percent of all commercial production. Figure 10.3 includes the average production levels for the periods 1985, 1986, and 1987 for the major producing countries. The countries shown in Figure 10.3 are Brazil (BR), United States (US), Spain (SP), Japan (JA), Italy (IT), Mexico (MX), Egypt (EG), Morocco (MR), Israel (IS), Argentina (AR), Turkey (TK), Greece (GR), and South Africa (SF). The United States and Brazil are by far the largest producing countries, with each supplying over 7 million metric tons of sweet oranges. Supplies for the remaining countries in Figure 10.3 are led by Japan, Spain, and Italy. The major difference between Brazil and the United States reflects both the growth in Brazil and the freeze losses in Florida. Prior to the Florida freezes in the early eighties the first two

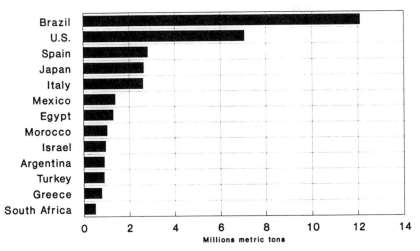

Figure 10.3. Citrus production by major producing countries (1985–87).

bars in Figure 10.3 would be much closer. As Florida continues to re-
cover from the freeze losses, these values are again likely to be much
closer in value.

Each column in Figure 10.4 shows the share of fresh utilization of
oranges. On average less than 20 percent of the U.S. supplies were sold
fresh. For the periods from 1981 to 1987 approximated 15 to 17 percent
of Brazil's oranges were marketed as fresh. In contrast, fresh utilization
was predominant for all other major producing countries. Around 42
percent of the oranges produced by the major world suppliers were sold
fresh, and Brazil and the United States represented less than 50 percent
of these. At the same time, Brazil and the United States supplied nearly
93 percent of the world's processed citrus juices. As evident from Figure
10.4, one would expect the institutional structures to differ somewhat
since the two major suppliers are primarily processed oriented while the
other leading producing regions are fresh oriented.

If the citrus is consumed primarily within the same producing country versus a heavy export emphasis, then the institutional structure is
likely to differ across suppliers. Nearly all of Brazil's fresh oranges are
consumed domestically, with only minor levels of fresh exports being
recorded. Fresh exports from the United States are slightly higher, ap-
proaching 22 percent. Approximately 50 percent of Spain's fresh supplies are exported while Israel, South Africa, and Morocco rely predominantly on fresh exports with minimal domestic consumption. In stark

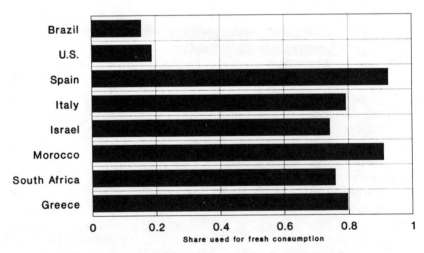

Figure 10.4. Share of each country's oranges used for fresh consumption
versus processed.

contrast, less than 10 percent of Italy's fresh supplies are exported.

When ranking these countries according to fresh export supplies, Spain ranks first with nearly 26 percent of the market and Israel ranks second with 19 percent. Spain, Israel, South Africa, and Morocco all rank above the United States as a world market supplier of fresh oranges.

Turning momentarily to the processing side, it has already been noted that the United States and Brazil supply nearly all of the world's processed citrus juices. As seen in Figure 10.1, the U.S. total orange supplies exceeded Brazil's for the periods from 1978 through 1980. Since then Brazil's total production has exceeded U.S. The major difference between these two suppliers is how the product is utilized and where the product is sold. Brazil processes most of its oranges and well over 95 percent of Brazil's processed oranges are exported, primarily to the United States, Canada, and Europe. Less than 10 percent of the U.S. processed supplies are exported. The reliance on exports both changes the internal market structure and the need for specific institutions. For example, expanded international promotions are a direct result of greater competition among producing countries relying on export markets.

Finally, before turning to the specific institutional structures it is useful to provide some insight into where the fresh exports are channeled. U.S. fresh exports to the EEC are relative minor. Shipments to Canada and Japan account for most of the U.S. export supplies. Spain is the dominant supplier to the EEC but does not depend solely on these exports. Israel, South Africa, and Morocco rely on the EEC markets for a large share of their export trade. What is most apparent is that while Brazil and the United States are by far the major orange suppliers, their impact on the world's marketplace can be significantly reduced depending on the types of products being considered. Clearly they dominate the processed markets but are considerably less important to the fresh markets.

Common Economic Objectives

The major producing countries face a number of explicit economic problems that have led to intense competition among world suppliers and greater cooperation and/or coordination among suppliers within a producing region. Likewise, efforts toward better coordination between buyers and sellers have generally occurred across the markets. In each country the primary method for achieving greater coordination has been through various types of institutional arrangements that either influence or completely control the production and/or marketing functions.

Common economic objectives that can be found among all of the major suppliers include:

- How to expand both foreign and domestic markets
- How to obtain preferential trade policies for exports yet protect their domestic industries
- How to improve both economic and technical efficiency. Technical efficiency relates to how well firms utilize scarce inputs while allocative efficiency relates to aggregate industry performance in establishing the economic value of their products
- How to maintain quality and standards necessary to remain competitive
- How to implement storage policies that are equitable and beneficial to the producing country
- How to assimilate and disseminate market information
- How to fund and implement research programs beneficial to the domestic citrus industry

While these economic objectives cut across all of the major suppliers, the methods for addressing them differ considerably from one country to another. The structure of orange trade depends on the patterns of imports and prices, the nature of production and exports, and the degree of governmental intervention in the marketplace.

Institutional Alternatives

The production and marketing of citrus require producers, processors and/or packers, wholesalers and brokers, and exporters. These individuals operate within what is called the marketplace or is sometimes referred to as the "vertical market system." It is within this system that production and product transformation takes place. Prices are set; products are allocated to alternative uses; storage decisions are made; product standards are established; and market development efforts are set into motion. Simultaneously, every country has a parallel legal system to provide the legal framework for completing all transactions. Market protection policies, setting minimal grades and standards, education, and public research and development are dimensions most often filled by various governmental institutions.

Using a simplistic concept of market and legal systems, private firms complete all production and marketing activities while the government is only peripherally involved in the marketplace. There is a clear division between the activities performed by the two supporting institutional structures. Within the marketplace we characterize the structure according to the degree of competitiveness among suppliers and attempt to measure market performance. On the government side reference is most frequently made to the degree of government intervention in the marketplace.

As the alternative structures found among the world's major citrus suppliers are evaluated, it becomes immediately apparent that market and legal systems are not fully separate or mutually exclusive. At a minimum the government provides some of the functions historically handled by private firms. For example, one or more government agencies may set minimal product standards or take on some type of generic promotional efforts. With this or other examples the interaction among the institutions is enhanced. In contrast to some overlap between private firms and government agencies, the extreme would be where the government completely assumes all the business activities normally completed by private firms.

Examples of this range of structural activities can be found among the major suppliers shown in Figure 10.3. The institutions facilitating both domestic and export trade among the major world producing states include marketing boards, marketing orders, governmental control, oligopoly control, and cooperative influence. One or more of these arrangements may exist within a specific citrus producing country. Government control refers to a structure in which the government actually maintains ownership of supplies and completes all selling transactions. Marketing boards control all selling activities yet do not retain ownership of the stocks. They attempt to provide a coordinating function through a unified selling effort through one agency. Typically, the boards are funded through a per box tax levied on all commercial production within that country. In contrast, marketing orders are legal arrangements whereby the industry can better coordinate the marketing of citrus through quality controls, promotions, and supporting services. In contrast to marketing boards, direct control over the selling transactions are not part of the marketing order concept. Finally, the selling transactions may be accomplished through a few large producers, packers, or processors who are of sufficient size to have substantial control over the industry. Prices and other marketing policies are set by a few firms making up the oligopolistic structure. In this situation there is strong price leadership among the packers or processors. Such strong influence on the market may arise because one or two firms have a large share of the domestic production. Likewise, coordination among producers through a cooperative arrangement may give a group of producers more power in setting prices and establishing industry marketing policies. In the next section details on how these structural alternatives are used among the major producing states are outlined with the primary objective being to give a perspective on how the world's citrus marketing is accomplished.

Producing Country Structures.   In the following discussion an overview of the more significant structural dimensions of each of the major world suppliers is given. The selected group of suppliers are included because of its importance and because it provides a cross section of the types of institutional arrangements that exist among the world's major producers.

UNITED STATES.   As noted in Figure 10.3 and in earlier chapters, the United States has historically been the world's largest commercial citrus producer and most of these supplies are consumed within the United States. Citrus production is concentrated in the states of Florida and California, with smaller amounts being produced in Texas and Arizona. As observed earlier, exports are important to the United States but they do not represent a major share of the total product movement. Hence, much of the institutional structure for the U.S. industry is directed to facilitate serving the domestic markets (Ward and Kilmer 1980). In the last several seasons substantial imports of Brazilian juice has led to significant structural change within the U.S. citrus industry. Historically, Florida processors have supplied the domestic market and were the only important importers. Since the midseventies more and more imports have been brought into ports outside of Florida where the bulk juices are reconstituted into consumer-size packs.

While it is difficult to categorize an industry as large as that of U.S. citrus, it can generally be considered an industry that is self-regulated with little governmental involvement in the daily marketing transactions. Basically, four structural arrangements exist to facilitate the product flow. First, there are in excess of 20,000 producers ranging in size from a few acres to large groves in the thousands of acres. Citrus production is highly competitive, with no one producer holding a dominant share of the supplies, whereas the processing stage is oligopolistic, with the top 5 processors controlling 50 percent of Florida's juice processing.

Producers interface with processors and packers in one of two ways. They may sell on the spot or cash market at the time of harvest or they may contract with the processor and/or packer. In contrast, a grower may be a member of a cooperative that both packs and processes citrus. Under this arrangement the producer commits his or her entire crop to the cooperative and receives an average price for the fruit based on the returns for the season.

Two institutional arrangements dominate the U.S. citrus industry: marketing orders and oligopolistic processors. Marketing orders provide the U.S. citrus industry with an institutional mechanism whereby the industry can exert some control over the characteristics of the products being marketed. Marketing orders may be federal or state orders. In the case of federal orders, producers within specific producing regions can exercise a limited number of controls on fresh citrus for that particular region including:

- Specify the grades and standards leaving the market order region
- Implement controls on the maximum amount of product leaving the region during designated weeks during the marketing season
- Designate periods during which no fresh citrus can be shipped
- Provide market support functions such as research, price information, and so on
- Provide market development programs such as generic product promotion

None of the U.S. federal fruit and vegetable marketing orders set prices or become directly involved in the buying and selling transactions. These institutions are only supporting structures that are facilitators to the trade. In contrast to the federal orders state orders can give the individual states considerably more power over the industries. For example, the Florida Department of Citrus is sanctioned under a state marketing order of Florida, which thus gives this institution powers to regulate the Florida citrus industry. Through the Florida Citrus Commission the industry can directly control both the grades and standards and support market development programs. At no time does the commission set prices or become directly involved in the actual exchange process. Like the federal orders, it provides a supporting function to facilitate both domestic and international trade. In summary, the Florida Department of Citrus and its governing body the Florida Citrus Commission limit their activities to the following:

- Establish minimum grades and standards for Florida's fresh and processed citrus
- Provide quality control through issuance of packing and processing license

- Fund a major generic advertising program
- Support scientific, economic, and marketing research
- Provide a coordinating body where various interest groups with the industry can exchange ideas and debate current issues
- Provide a clearinghouse for market information relating to both domestic and international markets

The actual buying and selling functions are external to the federal and state orders. All selling transactions are completed by fresh fruit packers and private or cooperative processors. There is no legal or formal system for regulating citrus prices within the United States. Likewise, there is no legal system other than through cooperatives where packers and/or processors can coordinate their selling activities. In fact, such coordination would be in explicit violation of the U.S. antitrust laws except for cooperatives. While no formal pricing agreements can be set among the processors and packers, a few large citrus processors can exert considerable control over the pricing process because of their dominant position in the market. Generally, one or more of these processors will adjust prices and inventories and the remaining processors will follow suit. This type of activity is typical of an oligopolistic structure where strong price leadership prevails. Even so, there is no assurance that other processors will follow, especially when the remaining processors do not particularly agree with the price changes.

In more recent years the pricing function has been more dependent on Brazilian policies than on oligopoly power of a few Florida processors. This loss in power over the pricing function among a few processors can be directly attributed to the growth in imports from Brazil to ports outside of Florida.

BRAZIL. Brazil is the world's largest exporter of processed citrus. Production has shown unprecedented growth in the last decade, with almost all of the additional growth being allocated to the production of bulk frozen concentrated orange juice. Unlike the United States, Brazil is heavily dependent on export trade. In 1983 over 96 percent of all of its orange concentrate was exported. Brazil also differs from the United States in that nearly all of its orange exports are in bulk concentrate (58 to 65 degrees brixs) while most of the U.S. exports are in consumer- and institutional-size packs. Hence, Brazil is supplying markets where reprocessing is required before the product can be consumed. Brazil's citrus production is generally competitive being supplied by about 5,000 commercial farms that are small, grower-owned groves. Usually 80 percent or more of the commercial production is processed into frozen concentrated orange juice (Myers 1978; Missiaen 1978). Two firms account for most of Brazil's processing capacity, and they controlled 7 of the 11 processing plants during the late seventies. In 1982 there were 9 companies with 15 processing plants. However, in 1982–83 three of the plants in the southern region of Sao Paulo did not operate. In 1979 the two largest firms accounted for nearly 75 percent of the total processing capacity and this level has generally remained true for the more recent seasons. Some growth since that date may have slightly reduced this percentage, but the industry still remains strongly oligopolistic with these two firms exercising considerable control over orange export policies.

As indicated above all exports are shipped in bulk concentrate form that must be reconstituted once it reaches the importing markets. Hence, the Brazilian identity of the concentrate is completely lost at the consuming end of the product flow. This lack of differentiation is in contrast to Florida's exports where the identity is generally maintained throughout the marketing channels. Sales are handled by the individual companies and are generally priced on a c.i.f. basis. Since Brazil is predominantly controlled by a few large processors who are capable of dealing in the international marketplace, there are no national or state institutions directly involved in the international marketing of citrus. The concepts of marketing boards and marketing orders have no direct meaning to the Brazilian citrus industry.

While the government is not directly involved in buying and selling transactions, considerable indirect effect on the industry can be found through subsidization programs, export licenses, credit programs, and tax incentives. Producers are eligible for subsidized credit to finance production expenses while processors can receive subsidized credit to finance investments in new processing equipment. Historically, processors have been given certain tax exemptions for exported orange juices, but this has been gradually phased out. The basic tax structure contains incentives that favor producers and exporters of FCOJ. Oranges processed in Sao Paulo state and exported have historically not been subject to the state levied value-added tax and have been exempted from some portion of the federally levied value-added tax. Profits made from exports of FCOJ have historically been exempted from corporate income taxes. However, such policies have been and are subject to rapid change. While the tax incentives and policies change continuously, what is important to recognize is that even though the government does not directly become involved in selling, it has historically provided substantial financial incentives to those processors who export orange juice (Wilson 1980, 15). The government has exercised control in that the Foreign Trade Department of the Bank of Brazil (CACEX) is responsible for issuing export licenses. This control can give CACEX considerable leverage over processors if needed. However, the larger processors have considerable input into the decision-making process within CACEX.

Unlike the U.S. citrus industry, Brazil through CACEX establishes minimum reference prices for FCOJ exports and for on-tree oranges to be used to produce FCOJ for exports. The reference price sets the lowest price that can be paid by the processor to the grower for fruit. The price is fixed for the entire season and is usually established in May and June. Because of the highly concentrated nature of the processing sector, the reference price becomes the price offered by all processors for fruit (Myers 1978, 17).

In summary, Brazil's citrus industry is dynamic and growing. The government provides strong incentives to trade but is not directly involved in the buying and selling functions. Trade transactions are predominantly directed through a strong oligopolistic structure from one or two large processors. Marketing programs such as international advertising, purchasing incentives, and varieties in packaging are not part of the Brazilian citrus program as it currently stands.

SPAIN. Spain is the world's largest exporter of fresh citrus and has been a progressive competitor in many of the major consuming markets and especially in the EEC. In general, the Spanish citrus industry is highly efficient resulting from the use of modern control methods for storage, fungicide applications, commercial degreening, and others. The industry remains predominantly fresh oriented as illustrated in Figures 10.3 and 10.4, and nearly 50 percent of these fresh supplies are exported. The structure of the industry is generally competitive at the production level. Fruit is harvested and shipped to packinghouses who in turn prepare fruit for both domestic and export markets. Recent estimates indicate that over 500 citrus exporters exist in Spain of which 10 percent handle most of the business. A trend toward some concentration in the export business has taken place, since only a few years ago there were nearly 1,000 exporters in the country (Traeger 1982, 6). There are roughly 80 to 85 cooperatives in the export business and they are estimated to handle 15 percent of Spain's citrus export trade. Spain's processing industry in 1981–82 stood at some 25 processing plants of which only 9 were equipped to process a maximum of 300 metric tons of fruit per day. Citrus processing remains expensive and the processing continues to face economic problems. In 1981–82 only 50 percent of capacity was being utilized. Also, Spain's yields and brix rates are lower than Brazil's and Florida's, which makes Spanish fruit comparatively much more expensive for processing. The trade linkage is direct between exporters and the various importing buyers, with no direct government intervention existing in the exchange process. The Spanish government does not control the planting, cultivation, or production of oranges. Its efforts are directed toward improving the industry's productivity through policies including assistance with various pest control programs, financial allowances for tree replacements, subsidies for input purchases, low-interest loans for capital improvements, price support for diverting oranges to processing use, export tax rebates, and support for export market development (Moulton 1983, 16).

Governmental efforts to assist with export market development has been through support for the Spain Citrus Coordinating Committee. Approximately 20 percent of the rebates given for exported citrus is diverted to this committee which in turn is responsible for implementing promotional programs for Spanish citrus. The committee is made up of growers, exporters, and government members and is fully funded from the tax rebates. In this sense the citrus committee operates much like the marketing order system found within the United States. However, the committee does not have control over grades and standards usually associated with the U.S. federal marketing order system. Market promotion activities by the Citrus Coordinating Committee totaled 230 million pesetas in 1981–82 for advertising fresh citrus. The national trademark "Spania" is used extensively with apparent success and all projections are for these expenditures to increase.

In addition to the promotion efforts by the coordinating committee the Spanish government maintains a comprehensive export payment insurance coverage system. The so-called distinguished exporter certificate program is designed to encourage and improve the trading methods of firms that have shown a degree of specialization and consistency in their exports. The certificate program is primarily an honorary title giving some prestige to the holders. The insurance programs appear to have been of only limited usefulness to the industry. Finally, grades and standards are controlled by the Ministry of Economy and Commerce while strong research programs are supported through the university system and 11 or so regional laboratories.

In summary, the Spain citrus industry remains fresh oriented with no direct government intervention in the selling or ownership of citrus. However, the Citrus Coordinating Committee is responsible for promoting Spain's citrus in foreign markets and for providing incentives to assist foreign citrus sales. The industry is progressive and highly efficient.

ISRAEL. The Israel citrus industry has become one of the world's most successful citrus producers given its limited size and resources. Attention to fruit quality, packing standards, storage, and transportation efficiency along with an aggressive market development effort has placed Israel among the major competitors supplying the European and other markets. Israel has also become an important importer of Brazilian concentrate which is then reprocessed and exported. For example, in 1981 5,688 metric tons of Brazilian concentrate were exported to Israel. In 1983, 61.2 percent of local production was exported as fresh while 31.4 percent was processed. Detailed data for processed citrus are not available, but most of the available data indicate that over 90 percent of the processed citrus is also exported. Israel has experienced surplus processed capacity in recent years. The trend has been to concentrate processing in a number of larger plants rather than continuing the operations of smaller and usually outdated ones (Brew 1983, 4).

Israel is the first country in our discussion in which the government plays a direct and formal role in the exchange transactions for the industry. All local and foreign sales of citrus are handled exclusively by the Israel Citrus Marketing Board (CMBI). This board has complete control over sales, contracting for sea and land transportation, organization of the transport, supervision of sales, and advertising. The board also advises producers on production and harvesting practices (McDonald and Hillebrand 1978, 12). This arrangement differs dramatically from the U.S. and Spain marketing order concept in that the citrus board is arranging all transactions in addition to those functions typical of a marketing order. Private contractors provide the coordination between producers and the marketing board. These contractors, who are mostly producer cooperatives, collect fruit from the growers, pack in a number of packinghouses, and deliver the fruit to the CMBI. Harvesting is done by the growers either using their own harvesting equipment or through various picking organizations. The board provides quality testing at the packinghouses and continually evaluates the performance of the system. Usually the board fines packinghouses that fall below standards and pays premiums to those that exceed the standards (McDonald and Hillebrand 1978, 14). Growers receive substantial premiums for fruit meeting export qualities while discounts are applied to fruit sold in the domestic markets.

Citrus prices are neither supported nor subsidized. Rather payment incentives are based on quality and performance. Israel's government policy is embedded in a national plan for agricultural development, production, and marketing, and the CMBI is the primary instrument to implement these policies for the citrus industry (Moulton 1983, 18). Israel places considerably less reliance on direct grower subsidies than do other Mediterranean countries.

In addition to the CMBI role as the seller, another important function is the development of foreign markets through advertising programs. The board has succeeded in establishing a national identity for Israel's grapefruit with the trademarks "Yarden" and "Jaffa." Other programs include sending technical experts abroad, supporting tours to Israel by potential buyers and/or handlers, participation in foreign trade shows, and conducting overseas in-store promotional programs. In 1982 an estimated $6 million was spent on market development efforts. Most of the promotional expenditures have been directed to the European market with somewhat less effort in the United States and Japan. However, both of the latter markets are viewed with increasing potential.

In 1983 the United Kingdom and West Germany were the major importers of Israel's grapefruit and oranges. Problems with devaluation and weak currencies have impacted Israel's trade as they have for many of the world's major citrus exporters. These problems, while currently severe, are likely transitory with respect to the long-run viability of the industry (Brew 1983).

In summary, Israel's citrus is coordinated through a marketing board that has considerable control throughout the vertical market system from producer to final exports. National brand recognition is apparent in the world markets and the product is consistently of high quality.

ITALY. The Italian citrus industry differs significantly from the other major producing countries in two distinct ways. First, Italy has been a long-standing member of the European Economic Community and thus shares in the subsidy programs of the EEC. Second, the entire marketing system is dominated by many small family-run organizations, which raises questions about the efficiency level of the industry. Granted, large size does not necessarily imply more efficiency. In 1983 Italy's citrus production remained under 2 million metric tons of oranges. In 1981 orange production totaled 1.8 million metric tons, lemon production approached 0.72 million metric tons, and grapefruit remained under 4,500 metric tons. Production is generally completed by many family-owned small groves and packing is usually through small family-run packinghouses (McDonald and Risse 1978, 1).

For years efforts have been made or planned to change the internal structure to improve on the current inefficiencies resulting from the numerous small packing facilities. It has been this pattern of family-owned facilities that partially inhibits the expansion of Italy as an important world supplier of citrus. As noted with Figures 10.3 and 10.4, Italy's citrus industry is fresh oriented and consumes most of its own supplies. Exports are not a major element to the citrus economy. Quality controls and grades and standards are not regulated and enforced to the degree shown for the other major producing countries. Often problems with grades and standards lead to problems with supplying the fruit qualities necessary for the European markets.

The Italian industry does not utilize the marketing boards or marketing orders found among the other suppliers. Also, an oligopolistic structure does not exist among the packers and processors. Overall, the industry lacks the coordinated structure that is often observed among those suppliers that are aggressively developing their foreign markets. The major governmental policies influencing the citrus industry evolve out of the ties with the EEC. Some of the specific policies include (Nichols 1980):

- Provide direct protection of Italy's citrus industry through common external tariffs to discourage imports when Italian production is highest
- Set reference prices to protect domestic suppliers such as Italy
- Provide export subsidies for the export of oranges to non-EEC countries and penetration premiums to encourage exports to other EEC countries
- Provide funding for capital improvements in packing, storage, and the distribution system

These programs are directed to subsidizing the industry and are not necessarily designed to improve efficiency.

Since the Italian citrus industry is still predominantly a fresh supplier with small export programs, it is not evident at this time that the EEC policies to improve the industry have caused much effect. Italy's citrus industry remains atomistic with minimal direct government involvement in the buying and selling transactions. The industry is, however, directed through government subsidies and incentives to develop new markets and channel product to certain markets. Product promotions and national brand identities are much less apparent than evident for many of Italy's major competitors. Projections are that the industry will continue to operate with small processors and packers with only small changes away from being essentially a domestic supplier.

SOUTH AFRICA. South Africa is the only major citrus supplier in the Southern Hemisphere exporting large quantities of fresh citrus. Hence, while the industry may be small relative to some other suppliers, South Africa can provide citrus during the off-seasons for the northern suppliers. The industry is fresh oriented as initially shown with Figure 10.3. In 1983, for example, 73 percent of South Africa's citrus was exported as fresh fruit, approximately 12 percent was consumed fresh in the local markets, while 15 percent was processed. In 1983 total citrus production approached 638,050 metric tons, which represents a decline from the previous three seasons (South Africa Citrus Marketing Board 1978).

The South African citrus industry is organized somewhat like Israel's industry in that a marketing board is at the center of the industry's operation. The South African Citrus Board and the Citrus Exchange are responsible for marketing all foreign sales of citrus. The board is made up of growers, consumers, processors, and packers. The board sets policies while the exchange implements the board's actions. The board acts under a single-channel pool scheme. At present the board controls oranges, grapefruit, and lemons which are exported and those that are sold on the home markets during set periods. The board also conducts pools for the export of citrus during the variety season of each type of fruit as well as conducting pools for the local market during the periods each year when the single-channel marketing regulations are in force (Haviland 1983, 8).

Overseas sales are arranged to obtain set target prices if possible. On the local market fruit is sold mainly on municipal markets and direct to factories and distributors at fixed prices. In some situations producers are exempted to sell direct to consumers on roadside stalls and factories. In total the board and exchange activities generally include directing the marketing of all citrus trade, conducting pre- and postharvest citrus disease research, coordinating the supplies from packinghouses, setting pool prices paid to packinghouses, implementing market development programs, conducting inspections and quality controls, encouraging research and quality evaluation in the marketplace, and providing support data and market intelligence.

Fruit flows from producers to the exchange through an estimated 218 packinghouses and the exchange closely coordinates the activities of the packinghouses. Pool prices are set by the exchange in accordance with the average quality of the fruit and the packinghouses in turn pay the growers accordingly. In addition to the actual selling functions the citrus board maintains a successful international advertising program where strong national brands are now well recognized in the major importing markets. The citrus board's well-known promotion programs for its "Outspan" and "Odda" brands continue unabated. Financing of the market development activities is done through the export pool system where income from sales is pooled and expenditures deducted. These expenditures are not made public, but it is estimated that $3.1 million was spent in 1981 and $3.35 million in 1982 (Haviland 1983, 9). Also, the citrus board's "Citruseal" mark of approval is used by the majority of the citrus juice processors. This identification is again a method to provide a national brand identity.

In summary, the South Africa citrus industry operates under a marketing board structure in which complete authority is delegated to the board including buying and selling and quality control. However, the board and supporting agencies do not maintain ownership of the groves. Likewise, the packinghouses are private firms or cooperatives free to compete and negotiate with the exchange. The industry is progressive and innovative in its market expansion efforts even though it faces increasing competition.

MOROCCO. Morocco's citrus production was near 901,000 metric tons in the 1983–84 season with nearly all of the production being in oranges. Only minor amounts of grapefruit and lemons are produced. Most of these supplies are destined for the fresh export markets, exported primarily to the EEC. Morocco competes directly with Spain and Israel for the European market and often benefits from the supply problems faced by these competing suppliers. The USSR also is a major buyer of Morocco's fruit. Generally, the more uniform grades and standards are diverted to the European markets while the less uniform sizes are shipped to the Soviet Union where the demands for specific grades and standards are not as strict.

Two organizations are of significant importance to the Morocco citrus industry. First, the Office de Commercialization et d'Exportation (OCE) is a monopoly with complete control over all citrus exports while the Citrus Grower Association in Morocco (ASPAM) provides representation for the growers. OCE is responsible for imposing strict quality requirements on export lots, often at the protest of ASPAM and other grower representatives. In 1983 one estimate is that OCE culled 20 to 25 percent of the fruit initially intended for export. Grading of citrus for export is on both fruit size and color and premiums and penalties are paid in accordance with the grades. Growers often complain that they are not being allowed to participate in the grading process.

Morocco has a long history of government involvement in the citrus industry. In the early seventies the government took over some large citrus groves owned by foreign nationals. During that period former owners lost all benefits from the groves and eventually the official agency under the direction of the Moroccan Ministry of Agriculture became responsible for the groves. The linkage between growers and the export markets is totally through OCE. As noted, fruit meeting export quality receives a price premium. Producers receive an advance payment for their fruit based on the crop estimate. A second payment is made after the final accounting for the year. If fruit does not meet export quality because of problems at packinghouses the producers are paid for export quality but the packinghouses are not.

The government does not subsidize or set minimum prices. However, OCE pays guaranteed minimum prices for exported citrus and FRUMAT, a grouping of most citrus processors, pays set minimum prices for culled citrus. Rejected fruit is either processed or sold in the domestic markets. In addition to the OCE control over the internal distribution of citrus, it has responsibility for promoting citrus in the foreign markets. Promotional campaigns sponsored by both OCE and ASPAM show some evidence of increasing demand. While this is a joint effort, other problems continue to persist between the growers and the government. Some of the actions demanded by ASPAM included (FAS 1983, 13):

- Reduction or elimination of taxes on products and services
- Elimination of customs duties on imported items needed by the industry
- Elimination of taxes on export earnings
- Increased priority for citrus in the allocation of irrigation water
- Price freeze on production inputs and an effective mechanism for insuring that the freeze is enforced
- Improved port facilities and efficiency
- Development and implementation of forestry projects designed to provide less-expensive wood for crates and packing material
- Improved credit facilities for growers
- Greater involvement by the association in export-related decisions and contracts

In summary, Morocco's citrus industry is controlled by a state-ruled monopoly that has complete authority over the exporting, grading, promoting, and payments for citrus. It differs from the marketing board concept in that growers and other groups do not automatically enter into the decision-making process. In general, there appears to be more conflict between OCE and the grower groups than is found in the other citrus producing countries.

JAPAN. Japan has a long history of citrus production; however, the varieties differ considerably from those of most other producing nations. Japan is an importer of fresh grapefruit, yet it continually faces a problem of surplus production of sweet oranges and tangerines. Such surpluses have led to long-range production shifts to alternative varieties. As was shown in Figure 10.3, Japan is a large citrus producer with nearly 70 percent of the product being sold fresh. Only a small fraction of its citrus is exported (Kitagawa 1981).

The Japanese market parallels that of many of the world's suppliers in that producers are generally highly competitive and often act jointly in small groups through producer cooperatives. Beyond the grove level the market systems become considerably more concentrated. Domestic fresh fruit will move from the local cooperatives to the wholesale markets and finally to the retail markets. The retail markets include supermarkets, green groceries, and specialty fruit shops (Kitagawa 1981, 851). The wholesale markets are highly concentrated with one of two Seika Co. (wholesale companies) and a number of middlemen and jobbers being the primary buyers. These wholesale companies are the primary suppliers to the retail markets although some small amount of product flows directly from the cooperatives to the retail markets.

One of the most essential differences between the Japanese and other world importers is the unique role of large trading companies in Japan. Nearly if not all citrus imports come through the fruit departments of trading companies, Fruit Trading Co., or the Trading Department of Seika Co. These companies act jointly with the government and exert considerable market power when dealing with the world's exporters of citrus. Once the fruit enters the domestic markets beyond the trading companies, the product flows through the system much like the domestic supplies. Product standards are high and the quality demands by the Japanese are rigid.

Beyond the cooperative structure of producers the Japanese citrus industry does not utilize the marketing order and board concepts frequently found among the other major producing countries.

Overview and Conclusions

In the preceding discussions the major institutional structures used to govern the world's citrus industries have been identified. The citrus industries produce predominantly sweet oranges, hence most of those institutions discussed relate to the world marketing of oranges. However, the same structures generally apply to lemon and grapefruit production. Total citrus production has continued to increase at a reasonably steady pace in the last 15 years and oranges remain the major crop of economic importance. Grapefruit and lemon productions are important crops but reasonably small relative to oranges. On a worldwide basis North America accounts for 35 percent of the orange crop, while the Mediterranean countries produce 29 percent. The Southern Hemisphere countries supply 20 percent of the world's production. Over 53 percent of the lemon crop comes from the Mediterranean states while North America supplies only 26 percent. Southern countries provide 17 percent. Finally, North America accounts for nearly 76 percent of the world's supply of grapefruit followed by the Mediterranean share with 16 percent. The Southern Hemisphere producers supply less than 5 percent of the world's grapefruit.

The structure of the world's citrus industries providing the supplies noted above can generally be characterized as highly developed systems yielding acceptable qualities to a diverse set of markets. Relative to many agricultural industries, citrus production technology is highly developed and readily available to most production areas. Likewise, in most of the countries, the benefits from marketing programs are well recognized. In nearly every country there exists some type of institutional structure used to enhance the marketing of citrus. Nearly 72 percent of all commercial citrus production is covered by some type of advertising program, especially programs designed to expand the foreign import markets for fresh and processed citrus.

Finally, the major institutional structures directing the citrus industries were shown to be marketing orders, marketing boards, government agencies, and oligopoly arrangements. Approximately 60 percent of the world's commercial supplies are subject to the rules and regulations administered by the marketing order concept. Granted that order arrangements differ in substance from one country to another, the extent of authority does not differ substantially across those countries using orders as the governing institutional structure. In contrast, only 8 percent of the supplies are governed by marketing boards. Israel and South Africa are the major countries using this arrangement. The Boards differ from orders primarily in that Boards control the selling functions while orders do not. Both structures have some control over quality and market development. Finally, the other category accounting for 31 percent of supplies ranges from government control such as in Morocco to the Brazilian system where a few large processors make most of the marketing decisions. Other dimensions to understanding structure should include a detailed analysis of barriers to trade, relative prices, product development, and research.

While the structures can be identified it is considerably more difficult if not impossible to explain why the various structures have been adopted by the different markets. The use of the different structures must to some degree be related to each of the following:

- The size of the industry within each country
- Nature of the product in terms of its use for processing and fresh consumption
- Historical problems relating to marketing and quality control
- Political system and historical precedence within the country
- Degree of reliance on export markets
- Differentiability of the product
- Importance of the citrus industry relative to other interests within the country's economy
- Country's level of economic development
- Existing structure of regulation and control
- Questions of social welfare and equity between producers, consumers, and handlers

The mechanisms in place to distribute orange products throughout the world are diverse, yet generally highly organized. As with most agribusiness industries, the market structure reflects differing economic systems, cultures, and distribution of resources. In the short run most of the changes seen can be related to significant reductions in crop sizes due to freezes and/or diseases and to changes in consumers' preferences for specific product forms. The latter is readily seen with the growing demand for ready-to-serve juices in the U.S. market. Increased imports into the U.S. market have been mostly driven by these two changes in recent years.

When viewing the citrus industry from a much longer term perspective, changes are brought about through efforts to gain greater access to markets. Tariffs, quotas, subsidies, taxes, distribution costs, and quality control become paramount issues. There is little evidence to suggest that tariffs and other forms of trade barriers among the competing world suppliers will be reduced on a board scale in the near future. In fact, expanded membership in the EEC and preferential treatment to several citrus supplying countries clearly points to the contrary. Likewise, U.S. tariffs and other taxes reflect a strong commitment to providing protection for the U.S. domestic industry.

Technology continues to play a key role in the ongoing development of the citrus industry. Changing product forms, packaging, and the ability to extend storage life are important dimensions. As living standards change, a potential growing market for processed products is feasible. Recent access to new markets in the Far East could greatly change the world demand for processed citrus products. Internal structural change will occur as international suppliers compete for access to the new and major consuming markets. Potential growth in processing capacity in Central America may become an added factor contributing to increased competition.

Bibliography

Behr, Robert M., and Ronald W. Ward. "A Simultaneous Equation Model of Futures Trading." *Canadian Journal of Agricultural Economics* 32(1984):1–22.

Brew, William R. "Attache Report – Israel." *Foreign Agricultural Service,* FAS-154. Report Number IS3024. Tel Aviv, Israel, November 25, 1983.

Brooke, Daniel L. "Citrus Costs and Returns in Florida." Food and Resource Economics Department Economic Information Report. Gainesville: University of Florida, various issues.

_____. "Citrus Production Costs and Returns in Florida." Food and Resource Economics Department Economic Information Report. Gainesville: University of Florida, various issues.

Brooks, Thurston. "Citrus Reference." Florida Department of Citrus, Economic Research Department, various issues.

Brown, Mark G. "Florida Citrus Outlook 1986–87 Season." Florida Department of Citrus, Economic Research Department, Working Paper Series (no number), October 29, 1986, 47.

Division of Fruit and Vegetable Inspection. *Season Annual Report.* Winter Haven: Florida Department of Agriculture, various issues.

Edwards, Dick, and Tom Camp. "Estimated Cost of Packing and Selling Texas Citrus." Texas A&M Agricultural Market Research and Development Center Bulletin 87-1. August 1987.

Fairchild, Gary F. "Analysis of Florida Citrus Harvesting Labor." *Proceedings of the Florida State Horticultural Society* (1975):96–100.

_____. "The Effect of Buy-in Policies on FOB Sales and Revenue in the FCOJ Market." Florida Department of Citrus, Economic Research Department, unpublished paper. Gainesville: University of Florida, November 1972.

167

_____. "Estimated Florida Orange, Temple, and Grapefruit Production, 1976–77 through 1981–82." Florida Department of Citrus, Economic Research Department, Circular 77-1. Gainesville: University of Florida, June 1977.

FAS. "Spain—Citrus Annual Report." *Foreign Agricultural Service*, USDA. AGR Number SP3084. Madrid, Spain, 1983.

Federal Trade Commission. "Federal Trade Commission Staff Report on Agricultural Cooperatives." Washington, D.C.: U.S. Government Printing Office, September 1975.

Florida Canners Association. *Orange Utilization, Prices and Yield*. Various Issues (a).

_____. *Statistical Summary*. Winter Haven, various issues (b).

Florida Citrus Mutual. *Annual Statistical Report*. Lakeland, various issues.

Florida Crop and Livestock Reporting Service. *Florida Agricultural Statistics: Citrus Summary*. Orlando, various issues.

Florida Department of Citrus. "Implementing the Frozen Concentrate Orange Juice Pooling Acts of Florida." Florida Citrus Commission Marketing Order No. 105-601. Lakeland, 1974.

_____. *State of Florida Citrus Fruit Laws*. Lakeland, November 1971.

_____. Economic Research Department. *Citrus Digest*. Various issues.

Geerken, Forrest K. "Attache Report—Morocco." *Foreign Agricultural Service*. Report 154 (Rev 6-79). Washington, D.C., October 24, 1983.

Grierson, William, Will Wardkowski, and W. M. Miller. Unpublished Report, Agricultural Research and Education Center. Gainesville: University of Florida, August 1977.

Growers Administrative Committee. *Annual Statistical Record*. Lakeland, Fla., various issues.

Haviland, Guy L. "Attache Report—South Africa." *Foreign Agricultural Service* FAS-154 (Rev 6-79). Pretoria, South Africa, March 25, 1983.

Hooks, R. Clegg. "Estimated Costs of Packing and Selling Fresh Florida Citrus." Food and Resource Economics Department Economic Information Report. Gainesville: University of Florida, various issues (a).

_____. "Estimated Costs of Picking and Hauling Florida Citrus Fruits." Food and Resource Economics Department Economic Information Report. Gainesville: University of Florida, various issues (b).

_____. "Estimated Costs of Processing, Warehousing and Selling Florida Citrus Products." Food and Resource Economics Department Economic Information Report. Gainesville: University of Florida, various issues (c).

Hooks, R. Clegg, and A. H. Spurlock. "Estimated Costs of Picking and Hauling Florida Citrus Fruits." Food and Resource Economics Department Economic Information Report. Gainesville: University of Florida, various issues.

Hooks, R. Clegg, and Richard L. Kilmer. "Estimated Costs of Packing and Selling Fresh Florida Citrus." Food and Resource Economics Department Economic Information Report. Gainesville: University of Florida, various issues (a).

_____. "Estimated Costs of Processing, Warehousing and Selling Florida Citrus Products." Food and Resource Economics Department Economic Information Report. Gainesville: University of Florida, various issues (b).

Institute of Food and Agricultural Sciences. "Agricultural Growth in an Urban Age." Gainesville: University of Florida, February 1975.

Kilmer, Richard L., and Daniel S. Tilley. "A Variance Component Approach to Industry Costs Analysis." Food and Resource Economics Department Staff Paper 82. Gainesville: University of Florida, April 1978.

Kitagawa, H. "Marketing of Citrus Fruit in Japan." *Proceedings International Society of Citriculture* 2(1981):849–52.

Lee, Jong-Ying. "A Study of the Impact of Three Party Programs on European Demand for U.S. FCOJ." Florida Department of Citrus Economic Research Department Circular 77-2. Gainesville: University of Florida, June 1977.

Lee, Jonq-Ying, and Mark G. Brown. "Coupon Redemption and the Demand for Frozen Concentrated Orange Juice: A Switching Regression Analysis." *American Journal of Agricultural Economics* 67(August 1985):647–53.

McDonald, Roy E., and Ben M. Hillebrand. "Israel's Citrus Industry: A Highly Effective Government-Grower Effort." *Foreign Agricultural Service,* USDA, May–June 1978.

McDonald, Roy E., and Lawrence A. Risse. "U.S. Competitors in the World Citrus Markets." *Foreign Agricultural Service,* USDA, May–June 1978.

Malick, William, and Ronald W. Ward. "Stock Effects and Seasonality in the FCOJ Futures Basis." *Journal of Futures Markets* 7(April 1987):157–67.

Missiaen, Edmond. "Brazil to Set Orange and Orange Juice Production Record." *Foreign Agriculture. Foreign Agricultural Service.* Washington, D.C., September 4, 1978.

_____. "Citrus in Mexico." *Foreign Agricultural Service,* USDA, FAS-M-299. Washington, D.C., May 1981.

Moulton, Kirby S. "European Community's Horticultural Trade: Implications of EC Enlargement." *Foreign Agricultural Economics,* Report No. 191. November 1983.

Mueller, Willard F., Peter G. Helmberger, and Thomas W. Paterson. *The Sunkist Case, A Study in Legal-Economic Analysis.* Lexington, Mass.: Lexington Books, 1987.

Muraro, Ronald P. "Budgeting Costs and Returns: Central Florida Citrus Production." Food and Resource Economics Department Economic Information Report. Gainesville: University of Florida, various issues.

Myers, L. H. *Summary of Basic Issues Surrounding FDOC Three Party Programs.* Florida Department of Citrus, Economic Research Department. Gainesville, Fla., May 1979.

Myers, Lester. "The Brazilian Citrus Industry." Economic Research Department Report (unpublished). Gainesville, Fla., December 14, 1978a.

_____. "Update of Round Orange and Temple, Outlook as of February 21, 1978." Florida Department of Citrus Economics Research Department, interoffice communication. Gainesville: University of Florida, February 21, 1978b.

Nichols, Edmond L. "Attache Report—Italy." *Foreign Agricultural Service,* FAS-154A (Rev 6–79). Rome, Italy, November 28, 1980.

Nielsen Marketing Service. "Florida Department of Citrus Selected Citrus and Other Fruit Products" (bimonthly report). A. C. Nielsen, various issues.

Niles, James A. "Deferred Pricing—Cooperative." Food and Resource Economics Department Fact Sheet 19, Florida Cooperative Extension Service. Gainesville: University of Florida, 1977.

_____. "Deferred Pricing—Participation Plan." Food and Resource Economics Department Fact Sheet 22, Florida Cooperative Extension Service. Gainesville: University of Florida, 1979.

Niles, James A., and Ronald W. Ward. "Using the FCOJ Futures Market to Reduce Price Uncertainty." *Proceedings of the Florida State Horticultural Society,* November 1974, 287–92.

NPD Research, Inc. "Market Summary of the Beverage Category." Port Washington, N.Y., various issues.

Rausser, Gordon. "A Dynamic Econometric Model of California-Arizona Orange Industry." Ph.D. diss., University of California, Davis, 1971.

South Africa Citrus Marketing Board. *Thirty-Eighth Annual Report.* Pretoria, South Africa, February 1977 to January 1978.

Sunkist Growers, Inc. *Citrus Fruit Industry Statistical Bulletin.* Information Systems Department, Sherman Oaks, Calif., 1976.

Tilley, Daniel S. "Importance of Understanding Consumption Dynamics in Market Recovery Periods." *Southern Journal of Agricultural Economics* 11, No. 2 (December 1979):41–46.

Tilley, Daniel S., and James A. Niles. "The Impact of Sales of FCOJ in Large Containers on the Florida Citrus Industry." *Proceedings of the Florida State Horticultural Society,* 1975, 285–88.

Traeger, Fred W. "Attache Report—Spain." *Foreign Agricultural Service,* FAS-154 (Rev 6-79). Report Number SP2077. Madrid, Spain, October 18, 1982.

Tuttell, Maryellen. *Selected Hedging Strategies in the Frozen Concentrated Orange Juice Industry.* M.S. thesis, University of Florida, 1987.

U.S. Department of Agriculture. *Report to Congress on Dairy Promotion Programs.* Washington, D.C., July 1, 1987.

U.S. Department of Agriculture, Economic Research Service. *Fruit Situation.* Various issues.

U.S. Department of Agriculture, Farmer Cooperative Service. *The Sunkist Adventure.* FCS Information Report 94, May 1975.

U.S. Department of Agriculture, Statistical Reporting Service. "Capacity of Refrigerated Warehouse Cold Storage." Various issues.

U.S. Department of Commerce, Bureau of Census. *1982 Census of Agriculture.* Washington, D.C.(a).

_____. "U.S. Exports—Schedule B Commodity by Country—Domestic Merchandise." Report FT 410. Washington, D.C., 1963–1974 (b).

Utke, Ray. "Florida Squeezes Sunkist." *Business Week,* August 18, 1973, 84.

Wallace, Michael. "Citrus Industry is Independent, Individualistic, and Competitive." *Produce News,* August 1976, 3a.

Ward, Ronald W. "An Economic Analysis of the Florida Department of Citrus Advertising Rebate Program." Florida Department of Citrus, Economic Research Department, ERD Report 74-1, December 1974.

———. "The Economics of Florida's FCOJ Imports and Exports: An Econometric Study." Florida Department of Citrus, Economic Research Department Report 76-1. Gainesville: University of Florida, August 1976a.

———. *Evaluation of the Economic Gains from Generic and Brand Advertising of Orange Juice.* Gainesville: University of Florida, April 1988.

———. "FCOJ Futures Market Performance 1976–77 Season: Consultant Report." Food and Resource Economics Department Staff Report 68. Gainesville: University of Florida, October 1977.

———. "Measuring Advertising Decay." *Journal of Advertising Research* 16, No. 4 (August 1976b):37–41.

———. "Measuring Market Liquidity: Case Study of FCOJ Futures." *Commodity Journal* 10(1975):33–40.

———. "Notes and Analyses of Fresh Citrus Markets." Florida Department of Citrus Economic Research Department Staff Report 75-9. Gainesville: University of Florida, September 1975.

———. "Revisiting the Dorfman-Steiner Statistical Advertising Theorem: An Application to the Processed Grapefruit Industry." *American Journal of Agricultural Economics* 57, No. 3 (August 1975):500–504.

Ward, Ronald W., and Charles Smoleny. "The Market Structure of Florida Fresh Grapefruit Packers: An Application of Markov Chain Analyses." Florida Department of Citrus, Economics Research Department Report 73-1. Gainesville: University of Florida, February 1973.

Ward, Ronald W., and Daniel S. Tilley. "Time Varying Parameters with Random Components: The Orange Juice Industry." *Southern Journal of Agricultural Economics* 12 (December 1980):5–13.

Ward, Ronald W., and Frank A. Dasse. "Empirical Contributions to Basis Theory: The Case of Citrus Futures." *American Journal of Agricultural Economics* 59, No. 1 (February 1977):71–80.

———. "Fathoming the Fundamentals in FCOJ." *Commodities,* December 1973, 14–19.

Ward, Ronald W., and James A. Niles. *Application for Continued Designation as a Contract Market for Frozen Concentrated Orange Juice.* New York: Citrus Associates of the New York Cotton Exchange, Inc., June 1974.

———. "Concentration in the Citrus Processing Industry." *Citrus and Vegetable Magazine* 38, No. 2 (October 1974):22–24.

———. "Hedging Strategies in FCOJ Futures." Florida Department of Citrus, Economic Research Department Report 75-1. Gainesville: University of Florida, August 1975.

Ward, Ronald W., and James E. Davis. "Coupon Redemptions." *Journal of Advertising Research* 18, No. 4 (August 1978a):51–58.

———. "A Pooled Cross-Section Time Series Model of Coupon Promotions."

American Journal of Agricultural Economics 60 (August 1978b):393–401.

Ward, Ronald W., and John Tang. "U.S. Grapefruit Exports and Japanese Trade Restrictions." *Southern Journal of Agricultural Economics,* July 1978, 83–88.

Ward, Ronald W., and Lester Myers. "Advertising Effectiveness and Coefficient Variation over Time." *Agricultural Economics Research* 31, No. 1 (January 1979):1–11.

Ward, Ronald W., and Marsha Tilley. "Industry Concentration: A Case Study of Florida Citrus Processors." Florida Department of Citrus, Economics Research Department, unpublished paper. Gainesville: University of Florida, 1976.

Ward, Ronald W., and Richard L. Kilmer. *The United States Citrus Subsector: Organization, Behavior, and Performance.* Monograph 8, N.C. Project 117. Gainesville, Fla., December 1980.

Wilson, John H. "Brazil's Orange Juice Industry." *Foreign Agricultural Report,* USDA, FAS-M-295. Washington, D.C., April 1980.

Index

174
Index